PRAISE FOR

THE BEST INVESTMENT ADVICE I EVER RECEIVED

"The most efficient, star-studded investors' guide available . . . an unbeatable collection of accessible wisdom, not from theories of the Ivory Tower or wannabe analysts but from those anchored in real experience and with breathtaking track records."
—JEFF SONNENFELD, senior associate dean, Yale School of Management

"Claman picks some very smart brains."
—*New York Daily News*

"Value-added advice from some of the world's richest and most famous investors. In this book, Liz does readers the ultimate favor of sharing that wisdom."
—RON INSANA, senior analyst, CNBC

"Liz Claman's book does what no other has accomplished: She's made the personal advice and experience of dozens of the financial world's most successful people available to the average investor."
—STAN O'NEAL, chairman and CEO, Merrill Lynch

"Great perspectives on inves
thing here for everyone."
—JEFFREY IMMELT, CE(

D1017716

THE BEST INVESTMENT ADVICE I EVER RECEIVED

Priceless Wisdom from WARREN BUFFETT, JIM CRAMER, SUZE ORMAN, STEVE FORBES, *and Dozens of Other Top Financial Experts*

LIZ CLAMAN

BUSINESS PLUS

NEW YORK   BOSTON

Business Plus
Hachette Book Group USA
237 Park Avenue
New York, NY 10017

Visit our Web site at www.HachetteBookGroupUSA.com.

Printed in the United States of America

Originally published in hardcover by Hachette Book Group USA.
First Trade Edition: November 2007
10 9 8 7 6 5 4 3 2 1

Business Plus is an imprint of Grand Central Publishing.
The Business Plus name and logo is a trademark of Hachette Book Group USA, Inc.

Library of Congress Control Number: 2006923054
ISBN 978-0-446-69610-4 (pbk.)

Book design and text composition by L&G McRee

For Gabrielle and Julian

What makes the battle worth the fighting?
What makes the mountain worth the climb?
What makes the question worth the asking?
The reason worth the rhyme?
Someone to strive for, do or die for,
I have you Two.

"You Two"
RICHARD M. AND ROBERT B. SHERMAN

ACKNOWLEDGMENTS

This book would not exist if it were not for Bill Adler of Bill Adler Books, who sought me out and said, "You really ought to do this book." My heartfelt thanks to the incomparable and amazingly talented Dana Beck of Gravity Books, who provided guidance, patience, and support every step of the way. To Rick Wolff, my editor at Warner Books, who lit a fire under me just when I needed it most. To Warner Books for taking a chance on me. My gratitude to my dear colleagues Bob O'Brien and Brad Goode, who stood on the sidelines cheering me on through thick and thin. Bob and Suzanne Wright get all the thanks in the world for helping me to grow at CNBC and for providing such solid support. And a big thanks to CNBC for giving me the most wonderful opportunities each and every day I've been here.

My agent, Ken Lindner, who has not only believed in me since he met me, but has been a true friend. Jack Welch, who, the minute I told him about the book's concept, started pummeling me with brilliant ideas, all of which I was able to incorporate into the book. My heartfelt thanks to all my very successful but busy contributors for taking the time to share their state secrets with me and my readers. I am the luckiest person in the world to have the smartest, kindest, most generous man for a father. Moe Claman has been asking me for a decade now to write a book. Here it is, Dad. Thank you for inspiring me to reach beyond my grasp. My eternal gratitude to my frighteningly witty and dazzling mother, June. Mom, I hope you're proud. Thanks to my best friends: sisters Danielle, Holly, and Shoshana, and my brother, Brook, for all the love, support, and humor they've so freely bestowed upon me in late-night and early-morning phone calls across the continent.

But I owe the biggest debt of all to the shining stars of my life: my husband, Jeff Kepnes, and my children, Gabrielle and Julian. Everyone should be so lucky to have such brilliantly bright wattage lighting the path.

CONTENTS

CONTENTS

CONTENTS

CONTENTS

CONTENTS

CONTENTS

FOREWORD

Liz Claman has performed a great public service in convincing many of this generation's leading investors to share their thoughts on how to be a successful investor. There are nearly seventy individual contributions in this collection. They are readable and individually valuable, and together, they strike recurring themes.

Underlying all of those themes is the objective of capital appreciation (growing your savings) and the power of compound interest. It is startling to know that a $23,000 investment at birth, invested at a 6 percent annual interest rate, would grow to $1,015,334.35 at age sixty-five. Time and compound interest are magic.

Achieving any investment result first requires saving and you will find advice here to save early and consistently. And then you will find a variety of advice that is focused on capital preservation. In simple language that means, *don't lose what you've saved.*

Many advise asset allocation or diversified investing as a strategy to achieve the average market rate of return while avoiding the dangers of "all your eggs in one basket" or making investments without facts or knowledge, for example, taking a tip from your office mate or your brother-in-law.

Over the years I have witnessed otherwise intelligent and accomplished people make truly stupid financial decisions. I remember well a partner from a major accounting firm marveling that I paid taxes while he bought tax shelters to reduce his tax bill to zero. In a few years, his shelters fell apart and he was much worse off than he would have been if he had paid his taxes.

When I was Secretary of the Treasury I went to New York to give a speech and to do interviews with some of the big names in television news. While we were off the air, one interviewer asked me if I had invested in the dot-com bubble as he had. I told him no because I believe there is a big difference between investing and speculating. During the dot-com bubble there were many companies with billion-dollar market capitalizations in spite of the fact that they had no earnings—and in some cases no revenue. Most of those companies vaporized, as did the investors' money that had been put into them. This is a final lesson from this book: If it sounds too good to be true, it probably is.

PAUL O'NEILL
Former U.S. Treasury Secretary
Former Chairman and Chief Executive Officer, Alcoa

INTRODUCTION

The first time I ever heard about the stock market was in 1973 as a little girl growing up in Southern California. I noticed that every morning, my dad, a surgeon in private practice, would go out to the driveway to scoop up the *Los Angeles Times*, come back in, sit down at the breakfast table, and say, "Let's see how my Kodak did." He'd turn to the stock tables page, run his finger down the list of names in tiny print, and stop at Kodak. I had no idea what Kodak was. "The company that makes cameras and flash cubes," he said when I was finally old enough to ask. On some days he'd smile when he finally found what he was looking for on the page. On others, he'd frown and shake his head.

He explained what a stock was, that he

owned a handful of shares, that the price moved up or down each day, and that it was like gambling. "You only buy stock with money you can afford to lose," he told me. "Do you have to wait until the newspaper comes to find out what happened each day?" I asked. "Yes. *We* do," he said, adding with a wry smile, "but the big boys in New York already found out yesterday."

So much has changed since 1973. Today, anyone with a television or a computer has access to up-to-the-second quotes. The playing field has leveled somewhat, thanks to disclosure and the freedom individual investors now have to partake in this global Las Vegas we know as the stock market. But real success in the realm of investing still belongs to the very few, and that's why I wanted to write this book. I wanted folks like my dad to have access to the knowledge, investment philosophy, and style of those wildly successful few.

Thanks to my job as an anchor at CNBC, I found I had access to some of the richest, smartest, and most successful businesspeople in the world. I was eager to find out the best investment advice each contributor in the book had ever received and how it helped shape his or her own style of investing. Each person offers different thoughts and ideas that have worked for them. No one offers the perfect "secret sauce" that guarantees instant millions, but combine them all, and readers will get an amazing cross section of investment tips from people to whom they normally would never have access. For so long, Wall Street has been a secret garden to which only a privileged few had access. With this book, I hope to turn that secret garden into an open playing field upon which everyone can score.

LIZ CLAMAN

THE BEST INVESTMENT
ADVICE I EVER RECEIVED
FROM THE GREATEST
INVESTOR OF OUR TIME,
WARREN BUFFETT

I was anchoring my financial news program one day when I looked in the camera and announced to the viewers, "Billionaire investor Warren Buffett just took a stake in an Israeli company. Is now the time for *you* to be looking at Israeli companies as a good investment?"

If Warren Buffett were watching, he might have burst out laughing, or at least chuckled. And I certainly know why. If there's one thing I've learned in my eight years as a financial news anchor and reporter, it's that Warren Buffett buys *companies*. He doesn't buy sectors, "ideas," or fads. If he's considering buying a company—

or a stake in a company—he'll pick it apart like a kid sitting in a basement with an old transistor radio, trying to figure out how all the wires and tiny parts work. He didn't buy that Israeli company because he believed Israel is the "next big thing." He bought it because that particular company fit into his formula. And what a formula it is.

Over the years, I've keenly observed Buffett's investing style and had an opportunity to chat with him about the way he invests. He once told me that when he was nineteen years old, he read a book that changed everything for him when it came to investing. He was at the University of Nebraska in 1949, and during his last year of college, he bought a copy of Benjamin Graham's *The Intelligent Investor*.

From that book, he learned what eventually became his own three principles of investing, and he has followed those rules for decades. Simple stuff, as he called it. His most important principle is that you have to look at a stock *as being part of a business* versus something that has a lot of flash about it or something that your broker or neighbor simply tells you about.

Buffett looks at a company and carefully assesses the *intrinsic value of the business*. How do you do that? For starters, look into the company reports and filings that the Securities and Exchange Commission requires every publicly traded company to provide investors. After reading and studying it all, ask yourself whether this business is straightforward and understandable. Does it have cash flow? What are its long-term prospects? Are its earnings reports relatively consistent? Does it have a solid, consistent operating history? High profit margins? These are all important signposts Buffett reads on the road before deciding to invest in a company.

The truth is, none of this is particularly complicated or sophisticated, but very few investors seem to take the time to follow these simple steps. But Warren Buffett does.

Buffett's second principle involves the *investor's attitude toward stock and market fluctuations.* He once said those fluctuations are there to serve investors rather than to instruct them. Buffett believes investors should turn a deaf ear to the day-to-day gyrations of the stock market. Good quality companies can withstand these gyrations. Yes, they might suffer a quarter or two, but in the long-term, they'll stand tall and strong. Buffett's best manifestation of his ability to ignore market hysteria came during the dot-com glee of the late 1990s. He simply wouldn't allow the stock market hysteria going on at that time to "instruct" him to abandon his tried-and-true formula. Over time, it was clear that this was a solid strategy that paid off in spades for his company and his investors.

His third principle involves the *margin of safety*. That means, as Buffett once put it, you're never that precise in your ability to calculate the worth of a stock but what you *can* do is estimate. He has often said investors should find properties where there is a wide discrepancy . . . and if you can buy them at two-thirds of what they're worth, do it. How does an investor accomplish that? As you pick through company reports and filings, add up the numbers and ask yourself whether the price of the business (or stock) is lower than its value. In other words, if you can calculate that a company's stock is worth between $80 and $120, and you can buy it at $60, then buy it.

Year after year, Buffett bakes up his investment cake with the very same ingredients as the year before, with a sprinkle of humor tossed in. A perfect example comes from his letter to Berkshire Hathaway shareholders back in 1995 (Buffett, of course, is the chairman and CEO of Berkshire Hathaway, Inc.):

> Charlie Munger, Berkshire's vice chairman and my partner, and I want to build a collection of companies—both wholly and partly owned—that have excellent economic characteristics and that are run by outstanding managers. Our favorite acquisition is the negotiated transaction that

allows us to purchase 100 percent of such a business at a fair price. But we are almost as happy when the stock market offers us the chance to buy a modest percentage of an outstanding business at a pro rata price well below what it would take to buy 100 percent. This double-barreled approach—purchases of entire businesses through negotiation or purchases of part-interests through the stock market—gives us an important advantage over capital-allocators who stick to a single course. Woody Allen once explained why eclecticism works: "The real advantage of being bisexual is that it doubles your chances for a date on Saturday night."

Over the years, we've been Woody-like in our thinking, attempting to increase our marketable investments in wonderful businesses, while simultaneously trying to buy similar businesses in their entirety.

But Warren's so much more than the companies he's bought and sold. Warren Buffett is considered by many to be one of the so-called good guys of American business. He's the first to take the blame when his own company's numbers aren't up to his or shareholders' standards. In his 1999 letter to shareholders he wrote, "The numbers on the facing page show how poor our

1999 record was. We had the worst absolute performance of my tenure and, compared to the S&P, the worst relative performance as well. . . . Even Inspector Clouseau could find last year's guilty party: your chairman."

And he's always ready to talk about the mistakes he's made and the lessons he's learned. In his shareholder letter way back in 1989, he wrote:

> If you buy a stock at a sufficiently low price, there will usually be some hiccup in the fortunes of the business that gives you a chance to unload at a decent profit, even though the long-term performance of the business may be terrible. I call this the "cigar butt" approach to investing. A cigar butt found on the street that has only one puff left in it may not offer much of a smoke, but the "bargain purchase" will make that puff all profit.
>
> Unless you are a liquidator, that kind of approach to buying businesses is foolish. First, the original "bargain" price probably will not turn out to be such a steal after all. In a difficult business, no sooner is one problem solved than another surfaces— never is there just one cockroach in the kitchen.
>
> Second, any initial advantage you secure

will be quickly eroded by the low return that the business earns. For example, if you buy a business for $8 million that can be sold or liquidated for $10 million and promptly take either course, you can realize a high return. But the investment will disappoint if the business is sold for $10 million in ten years and in the interim has annually earned and distributed only a few percent on cost. Time is the friend of the wonderful business, the enemy of the mediocre.

The one certainty I've learned over the years about Warren Buffett is that he is anything *but* mediocre. His honesty, his obdurate opposition to business shenanigans, and his concern for his shareholders is so palpable. His three simple principles—so easy for the average investor to understand and follow—have made him arguably the most closely followed and widely imitated investor in history.

LIZ CLAMAN

JAMES AWAD

Chairman, President, and Chief Investment Officer, Awad Asset Management

I loved the stock market from the time I was a teenager. For three summers in high school and during one summer in business school, I worked in Wall Street research departments. In June 1969, I was graduating from Harvard Business School. In the spring I started looking for jobs and I ended up with two offers from money management firms. One was from a glamorous hot mutual fund in Fort Lauderdale—it was the number one fund in the country in 1968 and was growing rapidly by buying small-cap growth companies and flying around in a corporate jet. The other offer was from an old-line investment counsel–mutual fund company in New York. My dad, who was a longtime stock market investor, told me, "Don't trust anybody who is glamorous and flashy and claims to have a secret formula for making money." Reluctantly, I decided to take the lower-paying offer with the lower-key New York firm. A few years later, the Florida company was out of business, as were many of the companies in which it owned stock. At the same time, I had developed a rewarding career at the firm in New York. Thanks, Dad!

When I reported to work, I was assigned to be the assistant to the fund manager of a small-cap fund—my job was to do research. I was young and eager. My eyes were always out for a good stock idea to give my boss. Florida land development stocks were hot in those days, as the state was in many ways lightly developed. One day, I heard of a company selling at $10 a share. That was cheap, so I went over to see the president. He was smooth, dressed in suspenders, and smoking a cigar. He told me they were going to report $4 per share in annual earnings later that week. I went back to the office excited about finding a stock selling at 2.5 times earnings. The next day, that president called to tell me there was a big block of stock available for sale! I ran into my boss's office and told him about the earnings and the block of stock. He said, "If it sounds too good to be true, it isn't true." He turned me down. A few days later, the company reported a loss—not $4 in earnings—and the stock went way down. Thanks, Boss!

The late 1960s and very early 1970s were heady days on Wall Street. Commissions were high and brokers, with a lot of money at their disposal, entertained fund managers lavishly with parties, games, and trips. In 1970, I was fortunate enough to be named a portfolio manager. I was young, ambitious, eager, and hardworking. The head of the company advised me to look out for my reputation—"always keep your nose clean," he told me. Little did I know how much I would have to draw on that advice! I was single so I was frequently propositioned by female brokers—one even showed up at my apartment on a Saturday. But the big test came at a lunch. I was analyzing a company and the treasurer invited me to lunch. At the time, I was making about $27,000 per year. Halfway through the lunch, the treasurer told me that he wanted to sell several million dollars of the stock personally but if he put it on the market it would depress the price. He offered me $50,000 in cash if I would buy the stock for the mutual fund that I managed. I couldn't breathe! I started to sweat! I didn't say anything. I just got up and left. A few years later I read in *The Wall Street Journal* that he went to jail. Thank God I kept my nose clean!

I joined Neuberger in May 1972 and by early 1973 we were in one of the worst bear markets in history. It was a terrible time for America.

Vietnam, inflation, high interest rates, gas shortages, price control—it was awful. People my age had never been in a bear market. On most days, the stocks went down and clients complained. It was depressing and lasted for two solid years. During this time, it was easy to lose confidence in yourself and in America. One day, I was sitting in the trading room. Roy Neuberger saw I was upset. He turned to me and said, "Young man, always have greed when others have fear and have fear when others have greed." He was telling me to get rid of my emotions and buy stocks because stocks were cheap. The market was down to five times earnings—anyone who bought stocks then made good money. I remembered those words many years later during the Internet/technology bubble in 1999 and 2000. Everyone had greed so I got some fear in me and avoided those stocks, which saved the clients of Awad Asset Management a lot of money.

Another important piece of advice is to always keep the relationship with the client. At one point in 1980, I decided to try to start a money management firm—I was tired of working for others. There was an institutional research firm that had no money management. The plan was that I would start the money management firm as a subsidiary and control it. I told a friend what I was going to do and he said if I was going to do all the work I should make sure that it was I who kept the relationship with the clients in case anything ever happened to the parent research firm. Over the years, I built a respectable small-cap asset management group. There were good and bad times but we did fine. At the same time, the fortunes of the parent company gradually eroded and I lost confidence in the abilities and ethics of the senior management. I could not turn fifty years old working in this situation so I decided to start Awad Asset Management, which I did in 1992. Most of the clients came with me so the firm was a success. Making that move and truly starting my own firm was the single best thing I have done in my almost forty years in this business!

Stanley M. Bergman

**Chairman and Chief Executive Officer,
Henry Schein, Inc.**

As the Chairman and Chief Executive Officer of a successful Fortune 500 company, it is understandable that people might assume that I personally know a great deal about making good investments. But what I have learned in my career is the wisdom of seeking out a team of expert advisors covering every facet of business—from marketing to finance to logistics—weighing their guidance, and usually taking their advice. Proof of the effectiveness of this approach is best seen in the growth of Henry Schein, Inc.

I use this same approach when making investments—I engage professional advisors with a proven track record of success to find the answers to meet my investment goals, and I listen to their counsel.

Looking back at the advice I have received over the years, I've identified three characteristics that successful companies seem to share:

First, invest in companies that are in good markets. A company is only as healthy as the markets it serves, and there should be numerous opportunities for future growth. Study the demographic trends that might drive growth, such as an aging population or an increase in discretionary income. And be sure the company is well balanced in its offerings to better weather temporary downturns in one or more market segments.

Second, invest in companies that have a great culture, great people, and great values. Of a company's many assets, the most important is its people—the values they live by and the culture they create together. Listen to what a company says about its people and what the employees say about the company. Read their guidelines for how they conduct business to see if they "walk the talk." Look for companies that include a cohesive team working toward a clear and common mission rather than a collection of individuals with diverse goals.

Third, invest in companies that are constantly reinventing themselves. Markets are changing faster today than at any previous time in history. We live in an era of instantaneous worldwide communications and a global market that never closes. New opportunities are emerging at record rates, and some long-established areas of profit are becoming obsolete. The companies that will be tomorrow's market leaders are those that constantly turn a critical eye inward and reinvent themselves to better serve evolving or emerging markets.

These three attributes are the foundation for a good long-term investment strategy.

RICHARD BERNSTEIN

Chief U.S. Strategist, Merrill Lynch & Co.

My father was not an investment professional; in fact he was a well-known research organic chemist, but he had a true Depression-era mentality about saving and he gave me the best investment advice I ever received. His advice was remarkably simple: Save. Save a lot and save often.

Now that might sound ridiculously simple, but how many Americans today are actually saving? My colleagues and I at Merrill Lynch have written extensively that we feel that Americans are not saving enough. The country could potentially be on the verge of a savings crisis.

One of the unique characteristics of Americans is that we generally don't realize that savings and consumption are mutually exclusive. You simply can't do both. If you ask the average American whether they are saving for retirement, they will undoubtedly answer yes. However, if their credit card balance is more than their annual allotted savings, then they are actually dis-saving for retirement. Their credit card balances might be compounding at 9 percent per year, whereas their investments might be compounding at 8 percent per year. In other words, they are "saving" at an interest rate of −1 percent per year!

Debt is an insidious detractor from building long-term wealth. It can give an illusion of wealth that isn't there, but the reality is that debt allows future consumption today. My father was wise enough to realize that if you live for today, then you have less for tomorrow.

This desire to consume at the expense of savings appears in many aspects of the investment process. For example, every financial planner today has an asset allocation model. The investor enters into the model for his or her expected future liabilities (e.g., paying for college, retiring with a certain income stream) and takes into account how much the investor wants to save, or can save, during each period into the future. Because the models are based on historical returns, and because investors don't want to constrain consumption in order to save, these models nearly uniformly decide that the riskiest asset class, stocks, is the asset class of choice because they have returned the most over the past fifty years. We've all been told a million times that we can't get superior returns without taking more risk.

Of course, in our hearts we all know that the best way to save for the future is to save twice as much and take *less* risk. But if I save twice as much today, then that would mean that I can't buy the third SUV.

Even today's strong housing market is fueled by the same misunderstanding of the mutual exclusivity of saving and consuming. It used to be that people built wealth through the equity of their homes. Today, people speculate on the price of their home going up. Extracting the equity from your home to consume today is hardly saving for the future.

Despite what a professional financial planner might advise, you can't save *and* consume. It's an unfortunate law of economics. My father seemed to understand that relationship very well. If more people had asked my father for advice, maybe America wouldn't have a huge trade deficit, a housing bubble, and be on the verge of a savings crisis.

SCOTT BLACK

Founder and President,
Delphi Management, Inc.

During the summer of 1966, I was living in
Maine. I did not know much about investing so
my mother sent me into H. C. Wainwright,
which was a research boutique. She knew a
broker there named Robert Lipkin. I did not
have much money then, so Lipkin gave me my
first piece of investment advice. He said the
smart thing to do was to buy a mutual fund. The
market had previously been killed that summer
under Lyndon Johnson, but I was lucky because
I had bought one of the Fidelity Trend Funds,
which had a good record. In the fall of 1969, I
went to Harvard Business School and sold the
fund, which turned out to be dumb luck because
the market got killed the following spring.

One of my classmates at Harvard, Robert
Goldfarb, gave me some great investment ad-

vice. After school, we both got jobs in New York. I went to work for Xerox and Bob went to work for Bill Ruane, who was Warren Buffett's best friend. That was when I was introduced to value investing, Warren Buffett–style. Bob explained to me that the key is to look for companies with a high return on equity and a low price/earnings ratio.

Before he became really well known, I was reading all of Warren Buffett's books and calling myself a Warren Buffett disciple. The key to Warren's philosophy is return on equity. You want to buy a good business. A good business is defined as one that generates a high return on equity with strong, free cash flow. I refined the criteria over time, but that basic principle still forms the nucleus of what we do at Delphi.

A big mistake people frequently make is trying to time the market. If you look at the rates of return throughout the twentieth century there is a clear message for individual investors—don't do it. Attempting to time the market is a mistake. You should have most of your money in equities, especially when you are younger, because this enables you to participate in the growth of the U.S. economy. The bottom line is that if you believe in the continued growth of the economy, which is a fairly good assumption, then you should be in equities. If you are holding excess cash and trying to time the market, you don't have faith in the long-term economy. Remember that compounding works in your favor over time. If you want to build wealth, you should definitely be in equities.

You should stay fully invested. You must be disciplined and forget what other people are doing in the market. Keep putting money away and give it to someone with a rigorous value discipline.

There is no need to invest just in the U.S. markets. I'd recommend some foreign exposure. Do not be afraid to take a look at Southeast Asia; for example, Hong Kong, Korea, or Singapore, but I would avoid Latin America and Europe, areas with huge social costs where the returns on equity are not very good.

Don't buy on margin—pressing your bets in the stock market by buying on margin is not a wise move. Finally, don't chase fads—when biotech stocks get hot, don't venture into them. It is difficult when someone next door has an instantaneous quintuple but you will make mistakes by chasing fads.

JOHN C. BOGLE

Founder, The Vanguard Group, Inc.;
Named One of *Time* Magazine's 100 Most
Powerful and Influential People in 2004

During the summer of 1950—even before my twenty-three-year tenure at Wellington Management Company and my subsequent thirty-two-year (and counting!) career at Vanguard—I was working at a summer job with a small stock brokerage as a runner, delivering securities to other brokerage firms around the city of Philadelphia. Perhaps to impart the wisdom of the lessons he'd learned, perhaps to mock the awe in which I held the securities business, one of the veteran "customer's men" (as stockbrokers were then known) told me: "Here's all you need to understand to succeed in this business: *Nobody knows nuthin'*."

After my graduation from Princeton University in June 1951, I entered the business, joining the mutual fund industry pioneer that managed the then tiny (but at $140 million, large for that ancient era) Wellington Fund. As I observed the stock market's daily ups and downs, as well as the seemingly futile moves of the fund's investment committee to select superior stocks and to adjust the fund's equity ratio in anticipation of the stock market's future direction, that early advice seemed right on the mark.

However hard all of us at Wellington worked, we provided a return for the fund's stock portfolio that at best paralleled whatever the market was doing, in fact lagging it more often than we led it. Similarly, whether we reduced equity holdings in anticipation of a market decline, or increased them in expectation of a rise, subsequent moves in the market proved no more likely to meet our expectations than to do the reverse. (In fact, the market seemed a little more likely to defy our expectations.)

As the years went by, my actual experience continued to prove that stock picking added little, if anything, to the returns we could earn on our stock portfolio, and changing the stock-bond ratio usually failed to add anything to the returns of the total portfolio. What was I to think? *Nobody knows nuthin'* seemed a serviceable principle that explained what I was observing firsthand.

In later years, however, it began to occur to

me that the problem was less that *nobody knows nuthin'*, but that *everybody knows everything*. That is, in an ever more informed and enlightened market, one in which stock prices were set largely by expert professionals trading with other expert professionals, most stocks were priced efficiently most of the time, discounting a wide range of expected future events. It followed, then, that betting on the ability of a given money manager to garner a substantial and sustained edge over other managers defied powerful odds.

As I considered the clear evidence of market efficiency, another, perhaps equally obvious, thought occurred to me. While all of that trading activity seemed to be a zero-sum game for the money managers, it was actually a loser's game. For what the winning manager *gained* from his knowledge and experience (or good luck) was never equal to what the losing manager *lost* by his lack of judgment and wisdom (or bad luck). No matter how it turned out for the buyer and the seller, the middlemen made money. They made a good living by being paid to manage the stock portfolios and to trade the stocks. Result: For investors as a group, after paying the large costs of our system of financial intermediation— likely around 2½ percent of assets per year— beating the market changes from a zero-sum game to a loser's game.

As I observed all of this focus on a "stock

picker's market" (never mind that, as long as each willing buyer is met by a willing seller, there is no such thing) and on the short-term moves of the stock market itself, I further modified my view. It occurred to me that those impulsive daily ups and downs were (after Shakespeare), "a tale told by an idiot, full of sound and fury, signifying nothing."

But whether *nobody knows nuthin'* or *everybody knows everything*, there is still room to be a successful investor, merely by understanding three simple concepts: 1) how to reduce stock risk; 2) what drives stock prices; and 3) how to optimize investment returns. This advice is of little value to short-term investors striving to know what is impossible to know or to anticipate, such as swings in the tides of investor emotions and the unexpected events that cause short-term stock prices to jump around so much. But for long-term investors, knowing these rules is the key to investment success.

Even though we know "nuthin'" about what individual stocks will do—in the next hour or day or, for that matter, the next decade—we do know something even more valuable: that the heavy risk of owning individual stocks can be eliminated by owning, in effect, the entire stock market—every stock, weighted according to its market value. When we do that, something magical happens. We eliminate both the risk of holding a particular market sector and the risk of hiring an investment manager who fails us. Of course the sector and manager may do well, or they may not. But if we can never be certain, we can diversify those risks away, leaving our capital exposed solely to the risk of the stock market itself. (That, by the way, remains a significant risk, at least in the short run.)

Of course we also know "nuthin'" about what the overall stock market will do in the short run. But we do know what drives market returns in the long run. The fact is that the daily, monthly, and even yearly (or longer) returns in the stock market are driven largely by speculation—paying more or less for each dollar of corporate earnings (the volatile price/earnings ratio). But in the very long run, stock returns are driven almost entirely by the fundamental factors of earnings growth and dividend yields. (As the academics correctly point out, "The price of a stock must equal the discounted value of its future cash flow.")

For example, if we add today's dividend yield on stocks (only about 2 percent) to the future growth rate of corporate earnings (historically, about 5 percent per year), we'll have a good idea of what to expect from our stock market. Of course, nobody knows at what rate, if any, corporate earnings will grow in the years ahead. But betting against corporate America is probably not a winning strategy.

So, if we know the value of diversification and if we have confidence in the ability of our corporations to produce long-term earnings growth at about the pace of our economy's growth, we can project a broad range of probable returns in the stock market. The only thing that keeps us, as investors, from earning those returns is the heavy drag of the costs we incur in participating in the market—the advisory fees, the investment expenses, the trading commissions, and the sales loads that imperil our ability to earn our fair share of those returns. If we know "nuthin'" about those costs, we're going to do badly.

On the other hand, as long as we realize that the gross returns that stocks earn, minus the costs we investors incur in participating in our financial system, equals the net returns we actually receive, it must be obvious that it pays to hold our costs to the minimum possible level. If the stock market's future annual return comes to a total of, say, 7 percent, why spend 2½ percent per year to get a net return of 4½ percent, leaving you with only 65 percent of the total? Particularly since nearly 100 percent of the market's return is there for the taking by simply owning a no-load, low-cost, fully diversified all-stock-market index fund.

When I first heard it fifty-five years ago, *nobody knows nuthin'* was great advice that pointed me in the right direction and explained a lot about the short-term realities of the market. But in the light of my half-century-plus experience since then, I realize that we do in fact know "somethin'." Not only that, but it is something very much worth knowing—expressed in a few simple and obvious truths, indeed eternal truths, about what we do know, as well as what remains far beyond the veil that hides the future from our sight:

- We *know* that neither beating the market nor successful market timing can be generalized without self-contradiction. What one investor wins, another investor loses.
- We *know* that *specific-security* risk can be eliminated by diversification, so that only *market risk* remains. (And that risk seems quite large enough, thank you!)
- We *know* that divided yields and earnings growth are the two fundamental factors that drive long-term returns in the stock market, and that's the beginning of wisdom.
- We *know* that cost matters, moderately in the short run and overpoweringly in the long run, and we can easily measure its dire impact. So minimize investment costs.

Finally, we *know* what we *don't* know. We can never be certain how our world will look tomorrow, and we know even less about how it will look a decade hence. But we also know that *not* investing is doomed to failure. So when we simply combine what we *do* know with what we *don't* know, we can illuminate the darkness that surrounds investing, and brighten our long journey toward building wealth.

JOHN W. BROWN

Chairman, Stryker Corporation

My best investment advice was received in October of 1976. At that time, I was contemplating a change of employment from E. R. Squibb & Sons to Stryker Corporation, a private medical device company based in Kalamazoo, Michigan. One of the directors, Burt Upjohn, told me that you accumulate wealth not through salaries but by acquiring equity. In my case, he was so right.

Subsequently, I agreed to join Stryker and prior to joining acquired approximately 5 percent of the company. That small investment in December 1976 has grown from a few hundred thousand dollars to a billion dollars. My actual return has been 34 percent compounded annually. Never, before or since, have I been given better investment advice.

SUSAN BYRNE

**Founder, President, and Chief Executive
Officer, Westwood Management Corporation**

When I was a young analyst in the early 1970s,
I worked with a strategist named Charlie O'Hay.
He used charts and economic cycles to help him
in his market calls. A student of market history,
he made me one also. I learned to focus on the
present in the context of the past. In other
words, *"the forest over the trees."*

In the mid-1970s, a normal valuation tool
was a stock's price/earnings ratio within its past
valuations, i.e., high end or low end of the five-
year range. The problem with this analysis was
that it didn't account for what was happening to
the *overall* valuation of the market. Because it
was a period of rising inflation, the valuation of
the entire market was contracting. Therefore,
valuing a company on its historic P/E range (in a
period of stable inflation) was the *wrong ques-*

tion. A great deal of money was lost due to this error in reasoning.

In the work I do now as an investor and as the CEO of a publicly held company, I am obsessed with attempting to ask the *right question.* That is the only way to get the *right answer.*

PETER S. COHAN

President, Peter S. Cohan & Associates;
Author, *Value Leadership: The 7 Principles
That Drive Corporate Value in Any Economy*

A very important piece of advice came from my father, who has been quite successful in investing. He always warned me against shorting stock. It is an extremely risky practice since there is unlimited potential for loss. If you short a stock at 10 and it goes up to 20, 50, or 100, theoretically there is no limit to how much money you can lose. You have to be very careful and you have to be certain you are right. My father's advice made me curious about the conditions under which shorting a stock could be a good move. A solid short opportunity arises when you can get some shares of a company that is headed for bankruptcy. If you find companies that are highly leveraged and in danger of violating their bank covenants because of industry and financial trends, you can make money shorting stocks. You just have to be very careful.

In almost everything I've heard that is accepted as conventional investing wisdom, you are able to find cases where it's wrong. Those cases can create interesting investment opportunities. There are some companies that don't look good on paper, but people like the story around them. Emotions get involved and the stocks go up and up, even though the companies' financials aren't the greatest. Taser, Krispy Kreme, and Martha Stewart are some examples of momentum stocks. People like the product, they like the person, they like the story.

The best thing to do for investment success is to identify the dominant trends within a particular era. There were basically two eras over the past ten years. From 1995 to 2000, it was the tech era, which valued intellectual capital and the Internet. In early 2001, there was a regime change in this country and a new era began. Clusters of industries like coal, oil, natural gas, defense, and certain conservative media replaced intellectual capital and the Internet as the new dominant trends. The sooner you can identify that there has been a change in an era, the sooner you can invest in it. Once invested in the new dominant groups of industries, the next step is to apply a competitive analysis to figure out which industry is going to do well and which companies within that industry are most likely to be successful. If you can do this early on in the era, you will have some excellent investment opportunities.

When you are researching companies to invest in, think outside the box. After Enron and WorldCom, I tried to think about whether there were principles that could come out of that to help investors. I wanted to know whether there were some general principles both investors and general managers could use to lead to higher returns. After researching numerous companies, I came up with eight value leaders. They were publicly traded companies that grew 35 percent faster than their peers in sales, earned 109 percent higher net margins than their peers, and had much higher stock performances than others in their industry. I found that these companies had seven common principles of value leadership:

1. Value human relationships: Successful companies believe that the way you treat your employees matters. If you treat them well, they will treat the customer well. Customers will come back for repeat business and a returning customer is more profitable than a new customer. Southwest Airlines is a good example. They have a rigorous hiring process and place great emphasis on teamwork. As a result, they are the only company in the airline industry

that has been profitable every year it has been in operation.

2. Foster teamwork: Goldman Sachs is tremendous at this. They recruit people who work well in teams and they will fire people who put themselves ahead of the interests of the firm. The company grew 45 percent faster than its peers.

3. Experiment frugally: Doing a lot of experiments to develop new products and services but not spending a lot of money on the experiments is the key to 3M's success. The Post-it note was created after an inexpensive experimentation process that a couple of 3M employees used to mark their place in the hymnal on Sundays. Today the company's culture revolves around encouraging this type of experimentation among its employees. Their stock price has grown 7 percent a year during the past thirty-three years.

4. Fulfill your commitments: In 1982, seven people died of cyanide poisoning found in Tylenol bottles. Johnson & Johnson has a credo that sounds very Motherhood and Apple Pie, but they actually adhere to it. Immediately, without waiting for approval from the CEO, who was unreachable on an airplane, the company recalled 31 million bottles, costing them $150 million. Today this

response is used as a model for how corporations should fulfill their commitments.

5. Fight complacency: The problem many successful companies face is that they begin to think everything they do is right. After a project, Microsoft conducts brutal postmortems involving 60- to 100-page memos. The memos are distributed to everyone, including Bill Gates, and they outline what the company did wrong and what they can do to improve. This culture of self-criticism and striving to be better is crucial and essential in fighting complacency and keeping the company moving forward.

6. Win through multiple means: Don't compete through just one capability. Compete through five or ten. This makes it more difficult for competitors to copy. MBNA is great at a lot of things—credit screening, training customer service people, market segmentation, and personal selling. Excelling on these various fronts made it the biggest independent credit card lender in the world, attracting the attention of Bank of America, which agreed to buy it for $35 billion in June 2005.

7. Give to your community: Though it has received a lot of bad press, Wal-Mart has given away $200 million annually to local communities for years. Much of the company's growth has been dependent on community in-

volvement. Every time it wants to open a store, the company encounters resistance from the community. Wal-Mart has gotten very good at understanding the needs of the community and trying to harmonize the community's needs with the company's desired growth. It has been able to keep up a rapid growth rate because of its ability to give back.

The implication for investors is that you should try to figure out what the value quotient is for a company you are looking at. Companies with high value quotients tend to do better in the stock market than companies with low value quotients.

HERSH COHEN

**Chief Investment Officer,
Citigroup Asset Management**

I came into the business in 1969. I found it easy to be bearish because the late 1960s saw furious speculation in stocks of questionable merit or creative accounting. Vietnam was heating up, the Federal Reserve was tightening credit, and the stock exchanges were dealing with paperwork crises.

What I didn't know was how to be bullish. In the summer of 1974, I was playing tennis with Larry Fertig, a man at least forty years my senior. He had been a syndicated financial columnist for the Scripps Howard newspapers, and had lived, and invested successfully, through all kinds of markets. He kept bringing me long-term charts of stocks that had suffered big declines but had fairly long periods of going down more slowly, or even being flat. He talked about bargains he was buying. He was very bullish on the market. Meanwhile, New York City was in trouble, the country was torn apart by the war, oil prices had soared, inflation had ratcheted up, and interest rates were high.

I said, "Larry, how can you be so bullish? There is so much negative stuff going on. There is so much to worry about."

He looked at me and replied, "Hersh, I have been investing since before the Great Crash. There is *always* something to worry about. The question is whether the *market* has already worried about it."

It was as if a lightbulb went off in my head. Those simple words of experience and wisdom have been enormously helpful to me in remembering to focus on how much the stock market has discounted, both on the upside and the downside.

P.S.: The Dow Jones Industrial Average was around 600 at the time.

ART COLLINS

Chairman and Chief Executive Officer, Medtronic, Inc.

Stay away from investments that you don't understand or that seem too good to be true. If an investment opportunity or a business has a strategy, a profit stream, or a financial structure that you can't figure out, or that doesn't seem sustainable, there is a very good chance you'll be disappointed over time. Pay attention to the organization's leaders, track record, and core values, and then ask the question, "Do I trust them?" Sound fundamentals equate to sound investments. If the fundamentals aren't there, don't invest; if the fundamentals head south, head for the hills.

John E. Core

**Associate Professor of Accounting,
Wharton School of Business**

When I started investing in 1990, a friend gave me great advice: "Read Peter Lynch's book *One Up on Wall Street.*" Lynch explains how he earned Warren Buffett–like returns as he originated and grew Fidelity's Magellan Fund. If you read this accessible and interesting book, you will learn much about investing.

But I will give you three more pieces of the best advice I have heard. I choose this advice based on what I have learned as an investor the last fifteen years, and based on what I have learned in my careers in investment banking and consulting and as an accounting professor at Wharton.

First, diversify your portfolio and minimize taxes and trading costs. This well-known advice on building wealth is unquestionably right, and is backed by over forty years of finance research. To diversify, I invest my entire portfolio in various bond and stock index funds. To minimize taxes and trading costs (and hassles), I invest with industry-leading, low-cost, high-service providers: Vanguard, Charles Schwab, and Barclay's iShares. Good providers like these leave you and your money alone.

Second, know your investment goals and choose your assets to achieve your goals. If you are like most people, you are saving for retirement, and you hope to retire in the next ten to twenty years. You have some cash saved in case you get sick or laid off. I encourage you to do what I do: Put a reasonable amount of rainy-day money into your state's equivalent of the Vanguard Pennsylvania Tax-Exempt Money Market. Invest the rest of your savings in a few stock index funds, either through Vanguard or by buying iShares. This is a safe strategy that will not go badly wrong. More important, it will give you very good returns over most ten-year periods. If, on the other hand, you are already retired or are building wealth that you need soon, you should invest much more in bond indexes and less in stock indexes.

Third, invest regularly and avoid timing the market. Over time, the stock market goes up 10 percent a year. But if there is a five-year return of 50 percent, almost all of that period's return can occur in one year. If you hold money in cash in the hopes of buying stocks cheaper later, you are timing the market. You will miss the big returns when they happen, and you will lose money. If you invest regularly, you will not suffer as I did from 1995 to 1999, when I tried to time the market and was in cash during one of the greatest bull markets in history.

To this great general advice, I add three pieces of specific advice, two of which I wish I had followed more often:

Save as much as you can, and your investments will do better. Investing mistakes can occur when someone has too little savings, and as a consequence that person tries to get too much from his or her investments. For example, someone has investments that are expected to be worth $500,000 at retirement (assuming an average return of 10 percent). But the person's expected retirement cost is $1 million. Faced with a $500,000 shortfall, the person becomes either too aggressive or too cautious. If you are not saving enough, you will have trouble funding your retirement. But if you have good savings, you can think of your investment returns as gravy. You will have more than adequate retirement savings, and you will retire well even if your investments under-perform. But if your investments outperform, you can retire early, retire better, and give some money away.

Do not pick stocks unless you are following stocks regularly. If you buy individual stocks, devote ten hours a week to following the stocks you own and to following the market in general. If you do not work regularly on the stocks you follow, you will do much worse than if you buy index funds. Remember that to make money, you have to be right twice: You have to start with a good buy and end with a good sell. I bought Kmart in 1990 at $13, expecting that the stock price would go up sharply when the company reorganized. The stock went over $17 when the reorganization was announced. But I was distracted, I neglected the sell, and I turned an easy 20 percent gain into a 40 percent loss.

Resist the temptation to sell stock short. Once you start following stocks, you will see stocks that you think are overvalued and will be tempted to sell them short (i.e., take a bet that the stock's price will go down over time). But when you sell short, you fight the 10 percent average annual increase in the market. And retail brokers typically charge you 5 percent interest on your borrowed shares. So if the stock's price does not change, you under-perform the market by 15 percent. Shorting stock can be frightening and painful. In August 1999, I became convinced that the Nasdaq was overvalued. I took a short at 2,750. The Nasdaq then shot up 80 percent to 5,000, and I lost 50 percent of my portfolio. If I had bought the Nasdaq instead of shorting it, I would have done better by 130 percent, which is a huge number.

To illustrate my advice, I have told you some sad stories about my own investment failures. The stories of my success are less colorful, but more frequent. When I have been successful, it is because I followed this advice:

1. The more you save, the better you will invest.
2. Do not pick stocks unless you are following stocks regularly.
3. Resist the temptation to sell short.
4. Know your investment goals and choose your assets to achieve your goals.
5. Invest regularly and avoid timing the market.
6. Diversify and minimize taxes and trading costs.
7. Read Peter Lynch's *One Up on Wall Street*.

JAMES J. CRAMER

Host, CNBC's *Mad Money*;
Markets Commentator, thestreet.com

The best investment advice I ever got was from my father, Ken Cramer, who told me that all that matters is inventory. If you have too much inventory, you are in trouble. If you have too little inventory, you are in trouble. If you have to pay too much to keep inventory, you are going to get hurt. And if you have the wrong inventory, you will get stung.

Of course, my father isn't in the stock business. He is in the retail box and bag business, the business of supplying retailers with packaging products to put their merchandise in.

It doesn't matter, though. As a hedge fund manager, I found myself constantly thinking about what my father told me. I looked at my stocks as if they were inventory and I recognized that in big sell-offs, if you are carrying too much inventory you will be annihilated. If the market ramps big and you are too lean, you can't catch up. So every day I balanced my inventory to be sure I could handle the next day's trading.

I also understood the dangers of credit. So many investors, including hedge fund investors, get enamored of credit or margin and do such silly things. My father had a total fear of taking down too much inventory through credit, and it transferred to me. I knew how to be lean when things were troubling and I never walked around with too much inventory as so many managers do today.

I knew my father never intended to make me a great money manager. He was just trying to do his best at International Packaging Products, selling gift wrap and fold lock-top boxes and plastic bags. But the lessons were learned and I am forever thankful for them.

MICHAEL CRITELLI

Chairman and Chief Executive Officer, Pitney Bowes, Inc.

I cannot remember a single source for the best investment advice I have ever received, but the composite statement from a number of sources would read something like this:

"If someone promises you a high investment return at low risk over an extended period of time, do not make the investment." If there were a single source that articulated this advice well, it would be a cover story in *Fortune* magazine about five years ago entitled, "The 15 Percent Myth." In that story, the authors contended that few, if any, large- or medium-size companies have sustained 15 percent earnings growth over a long period of time. Invariably, the growth rate slows down because the company gets too big to sustain accelerated growth, or it moves progressively toward higher-risk investments and makes a big mistake, or business conditions change to eliminate the sources of growth. A related piece of advice I received from my dad is that "If someone tells you that an investment 'can't lose,' there is a greater risk of losing money on it."

Unfortunately, I disregarded these wise pieces of advice in 1986 and 1987 when I thought no one could lose money on New York City real estate. My wife and I invested in two "can't lose" cooperative conversion deals and lost all our investment on both because of changes in the tax code and New York City statutes and building codes. Fortunately I later followed that advice and avoided losing money on dot-com companies because I did not believe that the high investment returns projected were sustainable or realizable.

DAVID DARST

Chief Investment Strategist, Morgan Stanley
Global Wealth Management Group

Paul Cabot ran Harvard's endowment fund for
over a decade. He said, "You have to get the facts
first. Once you get the facts, you have to face the
facts." Today, getting the facts is easier now than
it has ever been. If anything, we have an over-
loaded surplus of data, which can be challenging
to sift through. Facing the facts means stepping
back and seeing things with wisdom. Over the
great protestations of his colleagues who thought
we were going to enter another Depression,
Cabot radically altered Harvard's asset allocation
from all bonds and fixed income securities with
very low yields to stock investments. This revolu-
tionary move positioned Harvard's endowment
for a substantial upward move in securities prices
and the economy.

When he took over Harvard's endowment in

1948, it was about half the size of Yale's. When he retired it was double. Why? He faced the facts. People were expecting the servicemen and women to come back from the war exhausted and pass the time sitting in the garden reading the Bible. They were not expected to come back and be industrious contributors in the American economy. But that is exactly what they did. They returned, they had families and built homes in the suburbs, constructed highways, and bought things for their homes. Cabot had conviction. He had a willingness to take risks and to invest in the potential productivity of the postwar economy.

Taking risks is key to a successful investment strategy, but you have to take prudent risks. Think about your income and spending rate. What do you need to live on? Relate it to your portfolio, relate it to the risk you are willing to take, and evaluate it in light of the current market climate. While we work out of the grand excess of the 1990s, we are in a low-return world for the next few years. Look to the future—what will be the booming industries? Study demographics. The United States will have a tremendous population boom over the next forty-five years—even greater than China's. The Hispanic market in the U.S. will be hot. Research that area and find stocks that will benefit from this population change.

People need to look at their portfolio with more frequency. It is important to physically visit the office of your financial services provider. Sit down face-to-face and make it a habit, much like an annual physical with your doctor. Consider it a checkup for your portfolio. Another thing people need is an "Uncle Milton." This is a person who is wise, who knows you and your proclivities, who knows your mistakes and isn't afraid to call you on them. Your Uncle Milton should be financially savvy and sophisticated, but not in the investment business. Bouncing ideas off someone else can be invaluable. Warren Buffett has repeatedly said he would not be who he is without Charlie Munger. Everyone needs someone who will tell you whether your ideas are on or off.

If you are raising kids, take care of how you pay for college. Most people save like crazy—save for a house, then buy it. Save for college, then spend it all on tuition. By the time the kid is out of college, parents need to start seriously saving for retirement and most of their savings are gone. Consider other ways to finance school—loans, government grants, having your kid get a part-time job. Don't eat up your nest egg halfway through your life.

Investing is common sense. People think investing is brains and intellect, but really it is just sound judgment and common sense. Don't be afraid of investing—most people have far more common sense than they give themselves credit for. Pay attention to your surroundings, identify what the new trends are, bounce your ideas off Uncle Milton and you will do just fine. And don't forget to practice patience. We all have low attention spans—we want results and we want them now. This is when mistakes are made. All the investment greats go in with baby steps and with flexibility. When they start to see things go right they get the conviction. George Soros said, "It is not how many times you are right or wrong. I am wrong nine out of ten times but it is what I do in consequence of being right that has made my fortune." Knowing when to go lightly on the accelerator and knowing when to press it to your advantage will make all the difference.

BOB DOLL

President and Chief Investment Officer, Merrill Lynch Investment Managers

Back in the early days before I had any clue what I was doing, I was exposed to the options market. While I was at graduate school, I started playing the market and had a little bit of luck with a very modest amount of money. In the options market, you make a lot of mistakes because things come and go very quickly. The advice I got was "buy good companies." If you stick with good companies, even if your entry point wasn't that good, over time you will get bailed out because good companies eventually generate good results.

One piece of advice I give at seminars is very basic, but it is effective. Buy low, sell high. Everyone knows this maxim, but it's easier said than done. Few people actually do it. It is connected to the issue of discipline versus emotion.

We know historically that lows in the market are made when you have the most sellers, and highs are made when you have the most buyers and the fewest sellers. By definition, the average person buys high and sells low because that is where the crowds gather, it is what causes the panic extremes in the market—the big bear bottoms and the bull market tops. People should be buying low and selling high, but they are doing just the opposite. You have to ask, what causes that and what prevents people from doing "the right thing"? The answer is they forget their discipline and they get emotional. There is a frenzy when a stock is going up and people think, *I better get on the train before I can't get on anymore.* The fear of missing it is what causes people to buy too high.

Conversely, when individual stocks are going down, the temptation is to think, *Tomorrow it will be a little bit lower so I will wait to buy.* How long are you going to wait? Until it turns around and starts going up again? The emotions of fear and greed need to be tempered and replaced with discipline. And that approach should touch every part of your portfolio. For example, take asset allocation. You've got two asset classes—stocks and cash. When stocks go up and you have a target asset mix, stocks move up as a percentage of your portfolio and, using your discipline, you are forced to rebalance and to take some money off the table. Conversely, when they go down, the stocks shrink as a percentage of your total. Though it is incredibly hard to buy them when they go down, you are under your target allocation so you are forced to buy some.

An extension of this is the issue of success and failure in the investment markets. Obviously, there are no guarantees but as I watch the many investment managers at Merrill Lynch and others I've worked with, the successful ones tend to have a common philosophy, a process, a discipline that they stick to over time. Something that makes sense and works more times than it doesn't. The ones who aren't successful are the ones who don't have that sensible philosophy. Rather, they are always chasing the latest hot fad, whether it be an individual company or a particular methodology of investing that happens to be working at a certain point in time. The less successful people get on these bandwagons but by then it's too late in the game.

Listen to the market. The market tells you things. For example, you think you know XYZ Company better than anyone else and you are certain it is going to earn a lot of money, so you buy some stock in it. The next day, it goes down so you buy a little more. The day after that, the same thing happens. And on and on. Eventually you have to ask yourself, Am I missing something? The market is smarter than any one of us so listening to it is an important skill one has to have in order to win over time.

Remember that investing is part science and part art. The science is the discipline and the art is the judgment, the experience, and the careful listening to the market.

It is important to have an objective in mind. For example, you want to save money for retirement. First, get started. The magic of compounding says I can have a whole lot more later if I start when I am thirty than if I wait until I am thirty-five or forty. Second, if you have already started and you are concerned about whether you are going to get there or not, then invest a little bit more. Third, invest smarter. What is your time horizon and what are the asset classes that are likely to get you there more quickly? If you are saving for retirement and it is twenty years away and you have your money in cash, that isn't very smart because longer-dated assets, riskier assets like stocks and bonds, have a higher rate of return over virtually every twenty-year period than cash does.

STEVE FORBES

President and Chief Executive Officer,
Forbes, Inc.;
Editor in Chief, *Forbes* Magazine

My basic philosophy is if you want to get rich, start your own business. If you invest, pay more than lip service to disciplined investing and long-term investing. Everyone is a disciplined, long-term investor until the market goes down.

In investing, you should diversify—don't try to hit home runs. There was a wonderful money manager decades ago who said you should invest the way you play tennis. *Unless you're a pro, just try to get the ball over the net.* In investing, just try to get the ball over the net and let compounding interest do the rest.

One is always scared of unfamiliar territory, especially where even the pros have stumbled very badly from time to time. If you don't have time to do your own investing, to learn to read a balance sheet, and to learn about equities, then you should have someone else babysit the money for you through mutual funds. Go with an outfit that has low fees, like Vanguard or Fidelity. Put in a certain amount each month and don't worry about it from day to day.

There are two things about the stock market that people should keep in mind since emotions are so strong in this area. The bottom line is if it feels good, don't, and if it feels bad, do it.

In a bear market, the operative phrase is *going down the slope of hope.* In the 1990s, we had a long bull market and people figured that was the norm and that equities would keep going up 50 percent a year. In 2000, we had the big stock market hit and people wondered, *How long will this last? When will it turn?* Then we had a bear market rally, or a "sucker's rally," and people thought, *Oh, good, back to normal.* But there was another hit and another sucker's rally, another hit, another hit, and then people think, *Dear God, just get me even and I will never do this again.* That's when, if you have any money left, you should go in.

In a bull market, the operative phrase is *climbing walls of worry.* Everyone knows every-thing that can go wrong, but if you know it, markets know it, too, so when you look at the history of bull markets, there are long periods of time when people wonder whether this is a real crisis and whether these are real problems. For example, in 1997 the market got whacked due to the Asian crisis and in 1998 Russia's collapse smashed the market, so even in bull markets it never goes in a straight direction, you always have jags. In a bull market rises can happen very rapidly, then the market treads water for a while, so climbing the walls of worry is the appropriate phrase.

I was about ten years old when I first learned how to read a stock market table. My father cut a deal with me—he would pay the commissions and I could buy the shares for my birthdays and Christmases. One of the first things I learned was finding out what a dividend really means. The first shares I bought were in the Philippine Long Distance Telephone Company. It was listed on the American Stock Exchange with a pretty good dividend. But what I didn't realize as a ten-year-old was that the Philippine government took out a big chunk of that as withholding tax. And it was based on the dollar/peso exchange rate, which can make the dividend disappear rather rapidly.

I also learned to not always trust the experts. As with a doctor, you should get a second opinion. During my teen years, I tried to accumulate a handful of shares in Polaroid. It was a very high blue-chip stock that did extremely well. One day my father told me he thought Polaroid's rise was over and that I should sell it. I gave up two-thirds of the stock certificates and kept one-third back. He came home one night and said, "I talked to our experts at the office, the editor of the magazine, the chief financial officer, the investment guru and we all came upon a bargain stock that was undervalued so I put your money in that." The stock was Penn Central twelve weeks before it went bankrupt. So I learned about tax loss carry-forwards and tax shelters, but I also learned that in a disastrous situation like that you can make money from the ashes. Some of the securities that were issued in the aftermath during the post-bankruptcy restructuring did very well.

Sadly, the tuition you pay in learning about investing is not a one-time thing. You learn all the time. And that's why there's only one Warren Buffett out there. People give in to emotions. People get swayed when they hear at a cocktail party that someone made a lot of money and they think, *Well, I'm smarter than that jerk, I can do that well*. This is why discipline is so important. Put a certain amount each month into a low-expense mutual fund, diversify, and ride it. But you have to remember that investing is similar to riding a motorcycle. They are big machines and once people learn how to ride them, they figure they have mastered the machine, which is exactly when accidents happen. In investing, you should never feel that you really know it because if you do, that market is going to humble you.

In terms of investing your own Social Security, it will most likely be modeled after the federal thrift plan, which involves hundreds of thousands of people, many of them who know very little about investing, getting a choice of a handful of well-diversified funds, regulated for safety and soundness, which over time have given a far better return than Social Security has. During the early 1980s in Galveston, Texas, several counties pulled out of Social Security. They didn't even go into stock markets. They put the money into interest-guaranteed instruments from sound insurers, bonds, and CDs. Today those people are getting 50 to 200 percent more in benefits when they retire than they would have had in Social Security. These are not investment professionals. If you want no stock market exposure, you'll do better by having your own personal account than you will by staying in the current system.

The best advice I can give is don't put your money in a single investment, or a single company, or a single industry. Be well diversified. In bear markets, just ride it through, and as long as America is around, your nest egg will still be around, getting bigger and bigger.

DEBBY FOWLES

**Author, *The Everything Personal Finance
in Your 20s and 30s Book*;
Financial Planning Expert, About.com**

A lot of people simply do not know where to
begin when it comes to money issues. The
biggest hurdle for many people, the issue they
struggle with the most, is finding the money to
invest. You can't even think about investing until
this first step is accomplished. The best advice I
ever received was something both my grandmother and my mother repeated to me over and
over: *Save the pennies and the dollars will save
themselves.* What that means to me is that you
don't have to come up with a huge amount of
money all at once to invest.

You can find small ways to save and small
ways to cut costs. The thing people most often
ask me is how to cut their expenses and how to
have money for the things they really want. We

spend money without even realizing it. Get rid of habits like smoking, drinking, and daily lattes. These things don't seem like a lot but they can add up to thousands of dollars over a year. These habits gobble up money that could have been invested in a mutual fund. You don't have to give up all of life's indulgences, just become aware of your discretionary spending, track your expenditures, see where your money goes, and see how much could have been used for investing. People tend to buy the most expensive home, the most expensive car, the most expensive clothes, and the latest tech gadgets, but this is all money that could have been invested. You need to make a conscious decision regarding what really matters the most.

You don't need to be a financial guru to invest. People are intimidated by all the things they think they need to know, but they shouldn't be. If you are interested in doing the research yourself, check out Web sites like www.morningstar.com and become financially literate. Otherwise, if you don't have the time or inclination to do the research on your own, just put your money into a no-load mutual fund.

DR. BOB FROEHLICH

Chief Investment Strategist,
Deutsche Asset Management

The way I look at investing was fundamentally changed about twelve years ago when I was sitting in a pickup truck with James Walton, the son of Sam Walton. At the time, I was doing an investor conference in Bentonville, Arkansas. We were driving around talking about investing and he said, "You know, most people don't get it." "Get what?" I asked. "They don't understand the fundamental relation between a profitable company and a company with great service. Most investors don't look at this correlation, even though it is the leading indicator of a profitable company. Instead, they are too busy looking at price/earnings ratios and balance sheets, but at the end of the day if you can find those companies and industries that are really focusing on service, you watch what happens five or six years later. Good service is the best indicator. It is a qualitative way to look at companies and investment opportunities unlike anything else you tend to see."

At that point I started looking at customer loyalty, the types of repeat business the companies had, the way they were training their staff, the turnover of staff, trying to draw some qualitative things into a customer service, customer relations environment because this would mean they would have a more loyal customer base.

I consider myself a classic value investor. Before I invest in anything, there are a few elements I take into consideration. First, I look for a company that has a low price-to-earnings ratio. This is screen number one for whenever I've invested in anything. I do not want to overpay for what is out in the marketplace and I am always trying to get a bargain price.

Second, I am a dividend investor and have been for the last twenty years. I give my investment ninety days and every ninety days I look at things and I want my investments to give me some of what they earned. I want at least part of the story to play out every ninety days, in terms of the dividends. That has been the cornerstone of the way I invest—always looking for the out-of-favor, cheap valuations in the marketplace, and then within those I want the ones that have enough of a cash position to pay a dividend.

I think the biggest reason people are scared of investing and end up staying on the sidelines is that they confuse investing with playing the lottery. Too many people were chasing things in the late 1990s and the returns in the market got out of line. I watched sophisticated institutional clients sit there and extrapolate for me, "Now that the Nasdaq is up 80 percent I can retire in three years instead of fifteen years." Everyone forgot the tried-and-true issues of asset allocation. They forgot the wise advice of taking some money off the table after you make a profit. Many people are still not ready to come back in. And they probably won't come back until the pain of being out of the market is deep enough. When the market is flat, people don't think they lose anything by sitting on the sidelines. But if you look at things from a broader perspective over the last two or three years, you will see that you really have lost by sitting out. The problem is we want so much, so soon, and so fast. Therefore, it's tough to step back and realize this is a process, not a lottery ticket, and that you have to be in it for the long run.

BILL GROSS

**Billionaire; Founder and
Chief Investment Officer, PIMCO**

The best investment advice I ever received is hanging on my office wall along with the pictures of the two financial wizards who wrote them. They came from two autobiographies I read early in my career. The first came from Bernard Baruch, the famous investor in the 1920s and 1930s who reportedly sold out at the top and then gained influence in the FDR administration during the Depression as an economic advisor. The second is from Jesse Livermore, a speculator during the same period who reportedly made a million dollars seven different times and lost the same amount, only to blow his brains out in a hotel bathroom. Some role model, eh?

Baruch said, "Whatever men attempt they seem driven to overdo. When hopes are soaring,

71

I always repeat to myself 'two plus two still equals four and no one ever invented a way of getting something for nothing.' When the outlook is steeped in pessimism I always remind myself 'two plus two still equals four and you can't keep mankind down for long.' "

The Baruch quote is a classic reference to going against the grain when things get euphoric or excessively pessimistic. I've found that money is made over the long term by riding the wave of the crowd for 75 to 80 percent of the time. After all, the crowd is the dominant force in bull and bear markets and to go against it for a majority of the time would be like going to Vegas and expecting to beat the house! The crowd, in other words, has the odds in its favor much of the time if only because of its buying and selling power. As Baruch points out, however, you can't perpetually get something for nothing and the ability to get off the majority wave—even if a little early—is critical to preserving capital for the next bull market. The same applies to the jumping-in point during periods of excessive pessimism.

How to do this? Livermore says it best. "An investor has to guard against many things—most of all against himself." The secret to getting off and back on the wave of the crowd is to separate yourself psychologically from what is going on, to be hopeful when there is fear and fearful when there is too much hope. I think you can only do that by analyzing your own personality. Take an honest look at your weaknesses, how you react under pressure, whether you are an optimist or a pessimist, whether you are a risk-taker or a conservative, and so on. Write down your impressions and try to correlate them to prior behavior patterns in the markets. Put yourself on an investor's psychiatrist's couch with the objective of analyzing yourself within the context of the investment world. Then take that knowledge, along with Baruch's analysis of human nature, to help you to ride the market's wave for much of the time and to safely exit for the balance.

Lastly—another quote from Baruch—"Sell to the sleeping point." If you lie awake at nights worrying about your investments, you own too much or are taking too much risk. When you can go to sleep at night and not wake up wondering how the markets are going to open up the next morning, then you are adequately invested.

JIM HACKETT

**President and Chief Executive Officer,
Anadarko Petroleum Corporation**

The best investment "advice" I ever received
came from a personal experience when I was
twenty-three years old. It occurred before I knew
much about investing at all. In 1978, during the
summer between my two years at Harvard Business School, I was studying the cable and na-
scent satellite TV industry for a client. After a
huge amount of research, the client decided not
to pursue entry into this growing field, but I invested in the stock I thought best positioned to
win. The stock was Viacom. For two years after
putting my wife's and my savings into this stock,
it went nowhere. Then, I had to sell the stock to
finance our first house. Soon thereafter, it became a great stock. The lesson: Never invest in
one stock no matter how much you think you
know, especially if you cannot afford to hold for

a long period and/or cannot afford to lose the money. The portfolio theory of investing makes much more sense for the average investor, "just like the book says."

This holds true in business investing for capital projects as well. If at all possible, avoid making single-investment bets that risk the company's future if a cyclical downturn or project failure were to occur. While risk is directly related to reward in our world, risk needs to be prudently managed. As the world has advanced in the twenty-seven years since my first foray into investing, the management of risk has become an even more essential part of success, given the rapid change in technology, processes, attitudes, and information.

In making capital decisions, you want the best commercial and technical minds in your business to evaluate the two standard deviation (or 90 percent confidence level) expected outcomes up and down for the key elements of each investment. These elements should amount to five to seven critical factors determining a project's success or failure. Then classic risk management probabilistically calculates the mean outcome and tracks all decisions on these estimated outcomes. Post audits then lead to discussion, professional debate, and improvements in thinking and methods. Add to this process a relentless focus on investing in a statistically advantageous number of individual projects (or stocks). These constitute the magical process that allows successful companies to take on greater risk on individual projects while counterintuitively lowering their enterprise risk.

Most business success can be attributed to applying the best intellectual capital in a disciplined risk management model, as the above process suggests; however, I would add one element to this equation: The object of the investing has to serve others as an outcome of investment success.

The best of all investment advice is to invest in projects with an intent to sincerely serve others (employees, investors, customers, communities) and ultimately you will avoid hubris and emotion, preventing the spectacular failures and widening the chances of intelligent, humble success.

FRANK HOLMES

**Chief Executive Officer and
Chief Investment Officer,
U.S. Global Investors, Inc.**

I entered the investment business in 1978. My mentor in Toronto was a Warren Buffett disciple who introduced me to the way Buffett thought. What I learned from Buffett is what Buffett learned from Benjamin Graham. Using Graham as his basic platform, he created his own model in which he would pay a higher price/earnings ratio if the barriers to entry were high.

I started as a research analyst and then went into corporate finance. After that I bought a mutual fund company and managed my own capital, and eventually I became a chief investment officer. Throughout my career, I've been influenced by something Vince Lombardi said. He said you can never have a perfect game because you can't control the referees or the weather.

But, he said, you *can* have a perfect practice. Lombardi used to fine players if they were late for practice, because the most precious thing he could control was the practice process. When it comes to investing, the consistent practice of discipline comes into play all the time.

All great money managers are intellectually competitive, just like athletes. Many people get their CFA to be money managers, but in reality they are just paper-pushing administrators. They are academically robust, but they are not competitive and they don't have that extra edge, that driving instinct to reach the top. Warren Buffett plays bridge and Bill Gates once held his own Olympic Games. These guys are competitive. In reading books and talking to successful money managers, I realized they are all fiercely competitive. That was a common thread that related back to what Vince Lombardi said. I realized that because the market is so random, I had to focus on my process and be disciplined in the things I could control.

Another great piece of advice is something from Charlie Munger, who is Warren Buffett's partner. He believes that you have to work and think in a matrix. You have to have fundamental and tacit knowledge, you have to know people, and you have to take these different elements and synthesize them into a coherent whole. Look at how ants share information, and relate this to how markets share information. Look at how bees colonize, and compare it to how markets colonize. A diamond that has the most glitter has fifty-six different angles, so you have to look at something from many different perspectives. There is a famous school called St. John's College, where students spend four years learning nothing but the Aristotelian classics. Look at different models from an Aristotelian perspective and from a Cartesian perspective. Use different thought processes to review, reflect, and respond to things.

Pick one day of the week where you look at only macro issues, on the critical drivers of the global economy. Don't worry about the stock stories. Think about sectors of the S&P divided into ten different components and think about what is driving those, then rank them from best to worst. Update this every week for that week, for the month, and for the quarter, and ask yourself the question, *"Why?"* Is there new leadership? Is that leadership sustainable? What are the critical drivers historically? On the other four days you can concentrate on stocks and create a discipline where you only buy low-P/E or high-dividend stocks. Find your comfort level and create a model where you look at stocks based on five screens, which helps you remain focused and selective in what you choose. Time management is key and it is one of the weak areas for many money managers. By breaking down the process from macro to micro, from top-down and from bottom-up, you can allocate your research time more effectively. Then there is the integation process, where you strive to find great stocks that are in undervalued sectors in countries that are growing.

Another important factor is to appreciate the law of mean reversion. Everything eventually reverts to its mean. Markets will move above the average and below the average, so trying to time the market to get in and get out is a big waste of time. Appreciate the value of diversification and rebalance and catch the mean reversion. Follow the Roger Gibson theory of asset allocation. If you have 25 percent in bonds, 25 percent in internationals, 25 percent in domestics, and 25 percent in resources, then you have rebalance every year. Set an annual date for rebalancing and stick to it. On that day, evaluate your net worth and see where you are in relation to your goals.

From 1997 to 1999, the worst-performing sector was resources. Because the dollar was strong and all resources are priced in dollars, commodities were all weak. At the same time, the technology and media sectors were booming. If you had maintained that 25 percent rule, you would have been forced to sell your best-performing tech funds and you would have been buying these resource-based stocks on sale. Between 2000 and 2004, the resource position would have offset all your losses in your tech funds and you would have been net long positive. But most people did not do this and since 1999 they have lost money in their overall equity portfolios.

Susan Ivey

Chief Executive Officer and President,
ReynoldsAmerican Inc.

The single most important determinant in your investment strategy is to develop a thorough understanding of your individual risk profile and your long-term requirements and goals. And while it might be nice to achieve enormous returns on some highly speculative investment vehicles, you must also be prepared to lose just as big.

It is also worthwhile to investigate trust accounts to protect family inheritance but let the kids pay the tax! They didn't earn it to begin with.

A diversified portfolio of bricks-and-mortar stocks and bonds can deliver solid returns ahead of inflation without significant risk.

Consult professionals but understand the fee structure and the dividend reinvestment plans and utilize investment vehicles that recognize your retirement cash flow requirements.

Save young and use a 401(k) and/or understand your company pension while in your thirties, not in your mid-forties, when it is too late to adjust your own savings plan.

MIKE JACKSON

**Chairman and Chief Executive Officer,
AutoNation**

Call me boring. Go ahead, I don't mind. The fact
is, when it comes to investing, boring is a very
rewarding thing to be.

That's because smart investing is rarely
clever, and clever investing is rarely smart.
When I look for an investment, my goal isn't to
outmaneuver the next guy or apply some obscure form of technical analysis. Sure, there are
people who do that, who look at investing as a
battle of wits, but that's not why I'm putting my
money down.

I'm putting my money down because I want
to realize a reasonable return. And to do that, I
stick with the basics. I'm looking to own a company for the long term, so I want to see a business model that I can understand. If I can't make
sense of where their money comes from within a

minute or two at the most, it's not something I'm interested in.

Cash flow needs to line up with profits. The stock price should relate to performance. And the company should be poised for continued success by leveraging whatever advantages they have over the competition.

I'll be the first to admit that these are not the "Millionaire's Moneymaking Secrets" you see advertised on cable at two o'clock in the morning. My philosophy is not sexy, it's not secret, and it's not special. But it works, and the reason it works is that it's relentlessly focused on discovering companies that are committed to creating value.

As simple as it is to understand, though, it is often very difficult to execute. That's because the temptation is always there to be more speculative, to take a greater risk, to hope without evidence that a spectacular return is just a trade or two away. Resisting this temptation is one of the most challenging things you'll ever do with your money.

The fact that I've been able to do so has a lot to do with the people who first helped me understand just how exciting it is to be boring. Sometimes, it's not the lesson, it's the teacher— and I've been fortunate to have learned about business, about investing, and about value from some of the most intelligent, insightful people who have ever read a balance sheet. People like Wayne Huizenga, who made so much of his wealth in the decidedly unglamorous profession of waste disposal; Edward Lampert, chairman of ESL, who understands retail; and Dieter Zetsche, the DaimlerChrysler executive who first showed me how to apply an engineer's precision to business analysis. The principles I follow are the ones that they followed, and they're the ones that successful investors have been following for as long as there have been stock markets and balance sheets.

GARY KAMINSKY

**Managing Director, Neuberger Berman
Private Asset Management**

The two most important things we attempt to focus on every day are the power of compounding and the principle of "keeping your winners and selling your losers."

First, investors must remember that the frequently cited 10 percent long-term growth in equity prices is a result of one-half capital appreciation and one-half return of capital through dividends and distributions being reinvested. We always try to find investments in growing businesses that philosophically believe in steady and growing distributions to shareowners. My favorite story on compounding money comes from one of my three sons, Tommy. "If one is offered $1,000 a day for thirty days or $.01 a day *doubled* each day, which would you take? The answer is the penny.

The $1,000 becomes $30,000 while the penny is more than $5,000,000 over the same time frame!"

Second, human nature has us sell our winning investments (because we made a good decision) and keep or average-down investments that have declined in value. The greatest lesson of all is to *keep* those investments that you were correct on and continue to be growing and managing their companies in the right way and *sell* those that have failed. While more psychologically difficult to do, it will help preserve and create greater wealth!

BRUCE KARATZ

Chairman and Chief Executive Officer, KB Home

It is ironic that the best investment advice I ever received relates to homeownership. I can recall a specific conversation I had with my grandfather, who was my mentor, shortly after law school. He told me that buying a home was the single most important investment an individual or family could make.

"If you can afford to buy a home, do it," he said. He continued to tell me that rent is something that you will never have control of and can get out of hand. A mortgage is fixed, and even if the value appreciates at the rate of inflation, it will still produce a nice return.

A few years later, I was entrenched in the homebuilding industry and immediately developed a passion for delivering the American Dream to others. And after more than thirty years in the business, I pass along that same advice to customers and young families today.

As a leader in this industry, I understand the responsibility of providing these investment opportunities for deserving families, and understand that it is a unique investment in that people actually live there and enjoy it. As our economy and jobs continue to grow in conjunction with the increase in population and immigration, the need for housing, the imbalance in supply and demand, and the appreciation of homes in general will continue to rise as well.

Doug Kass

**Founder and President,
Seabreeze Partners Management**

The first exposure I had to the investment world was through my grandmother. Grandma Koufax was an original. She owned her own business well before it was fashionable for women to be entrepreneurs. She knew her way around a stock chart and was quite a successful investor. By the time I was a teenager, she had taught me how to track stocks and I kept the records of my imaginary holdings in a notebook. I was so interested in the market that I would spend my school holidays in a Long Island brokerage office watching the tape all day long instead of hanging out with my friends. While I was getting my MBA at Wharton, I made my first real trade. I bought a couple of shares of Teledyne—it went up nearly tenfold. After that, I completely immersed myself in the stock market.

Over the past thirty years in this business, I have learned a few things about human nature and how it relates to investing. Pride, impatience, ignorance, shortsightedness, and farsightedness can all lead to bad investment decisions. It is crucial to develop a variant view in putting together your portfolio in order to differentiate your returns from those of the majority of investors. Wall Street research is still steeped in group-think mentality; therefore, if you think outside the box your chance of having investment success increases. Learn to control your emotions. To win over the long run, you need to grind it out. Don't make hasty, panicked decisions. Trust your judgment and never, ever let your confidence be shaken. Pay attention to world events and trends. Then, predict how they will affect the stock market and how you can capitalize on them. Most important, when everyone else is doing something, you should not. The more certain the crowd is, the more certain it is to be wrong. After all, if everyone were right, there would be no reward.

ROBERT KIYOSAKI

Investor and International Best-selling
Author of *Rich Dad, Poor Dad: What the
Rich Teach Their Kids About Money—That
the Poor and Middle Class Do Not!*

At the age of nine, my rich dad began teaching
me to be an investor by playing the game of Monopoly. We would play for hours.

When I went home for dinner, I would often
break out my family's Monopoly game and want
to continue to play. My real dad, being a school-
teacher, would say, "Put that silly game away
and do your homework. If you don't do your
homework, you won't have good grades and
you won't find a good job with benefits."

A few days later, I would be over at my rich
dad's office, and he would set up the Monopoly
game and want to play. Being a young boy, it
puzzled me that one dad, my real dad, thought

Monopoly was a silly game and a waste of time. On the other hand, my rich dad, who was my best friend's father, thought Monopoly was an important game for my financial education.

Finally, I asked my rich dad why we played Monopoly so often. Smiling, he put his son and me in his car and drove us to a subdivision of about thirty homes. Stepping out of his car he said, "About ten years ago, I bought this land for nothing. Every year, I build three to four houses on the land and rent them out."

"So what does this have to do with Monopoly?" I asked.

Rich dad laughed when he realized I did not get the connection between the land we were standing on and the game of Monopoly. Smiling, he turned to me and said, "The formula for great wealth is found in the game of Monopoly. Do you know what the formula is?"

Still confused, I sheepishly said, "No. What is the formula for great wealth?"

Laughing out loud, rich dad said, "Four green houses turn into one red hotel. That's the formula for great wealth."

Still not getting it, I stood there nearly ready to cry because I felt so stupid. Standing on the land looking at the houses, I was still not making the connection.

Gently his son, Mike, my best friend, said,

"These houses are the same as green houses. That is what my dad is trying to show you. Someday he'll own a big red hotel."

Suddenly, the relationship between the game of Monopoly and my rich dad's life became clear. In a flash, I realized my poor dad thought Monopoly was just a child's game . . . while my rich dad was playing Monopoly in real life.

Ten years later, at the age of nineteen, I returned from school in New York for the Christmas break and went to see my rich dad's big red hotel (it was not really red)—smack dab in the middle of Waikiki Beach. In ten years, I saw my rich dad go from an obscure small-businessman to a major player in Hawaii's tourist market. Playing Monopoly in real life had made him a very, very rich man.

Today, my wife, Kim, and I play Monopoly in real life, not in Hawaii, but in Phoenix, Arizona, the fastest-growing state in the U.S. Just as Monopoly teaches us, we started small—with green houses—and, today, we are buying big red buildings, along the most expensive street in Phoenix, Camelback Road, right where the Ritz-Carlton Hotel is located, Biltmore Fashion Park (a very high-end shopping center), and the Phoenix offices of most of the financial institutions.

My investment advice is not about real estate or Monopoly. My best investment advice was my rich dad's advice on having a formula, an investment plan, and following it.

You see, real estate is not for everyone . . . and not everyone loves playing Monopoly. Yet everyone who wants to be a successful investor needs a plan, then needs to follow their plan.

One of the reasons why my rich dad loved the formula of "four green houses and one red hotel" was because it was a plan that started small and grew bigger. He would say, "Every plan should include a training period. The four green houses represented my training period, a chance to make small mistakes and learn from them. The big red hotel was my big dream . . . and every plan should have a big dream." To complete this lesson he said, "Start small and dream big." That is how my rich dad lived his life and that is the best investment advice I have received.

LAWRENCE KUDLOW

Chief Executive Officer, Kudlow & Company;
Host, CNBC's *Kudlow & Company*

I came up the Wall Street ranks from the Federal
Reserve. For many years, I was a partner at Bear
Stearns and I took over all the strategy responsi-
bilities for the firm. Ace Greenberg, a renowned
investor who was a longtime CEO of the firm,
once told me that if a stock falls five days in a
row, you should sell it. Never be emotional,
never get attached, never try to outwit the
market. If it goes down five days in a row, *sell it*.

I have taken that advice. Although I am not
an individual stock picker or buyer, I have taken
that advice when I look at macro strategies. If
the market is falling continuously for five or
more days in a row, it is sending a signal that
there is trouble. As a strategist, my job is to
figure out what the trouble is. The market is
never wrong. It is what it is. And it is smarter

than all of us put together. The United States market, which is the only true global stock market, contains the information of millions of buyers and sellers around the globe in its market prices. Whenever I hear economists or strategists say the market is wrong, I immediately think, *No, you're wrong.* I believe in the collective wisdom of market prices—the wisdom of all these people buying and selling. That is the beauty of price. It has tremendous information.

I do not think people should pick their own stocks. Most people don't have enough time in their daily lives to do the kind of necessary research, so there are two options to consider.

First, think about turning your money over to an expert—a mutual fund manager or a financial planner—who has a good long-term track record of no fewer than five years. Second, with the help of a financial planner, look into an exchange-traded fund (ETF). They are the best product to hit the market in the past several years. They are cheap and you have more tax control over them, in terms of capital gains and dividends. An exchange-traded fund allows you to buy baskets of stocks. Fifty or even 100 stocks can be in a basket, which enables you to be diversified. For the most astute investor, as well as the ordinary mainstream investor, ETFs are a great instrument. I like the concept of the Wilshire 5000, which essentially gives you a piece of the rock of all the actively traded companies. In effect, you are buying the global company as well as the American economy since American companies operate overseas.

The diversification concept is important to investing success because if you buy these large, broad indexes, you don't have to worry about over-performing or under-performing. Honestly, the trick is to hold it forever. I am not a trader and I don't believe in trying to time the market or outguess the short-term fluctuations. By holding on to your investments, you are making a bet on the long-run health of the American economy and our free market capitalist system.

Although we have stubbed our toes from time to time, that long-run bet on American prosperity has paid off very handsomely over the years, including through some of the worst downturns in 2002, in the 1970s, and even the Great Depression. Historians have shown that if you bought and *held*, you did very, very well. Your broker may be telling you to churn and your financial planner may be telling you to jump around, but don't do it. If you buy a piece of the rock, you are buying a piece of our freedom, our system, our way of life and it works out better than any other on the planet.

A. G. LAFLEY

Chairman, President, and Chief Executive Officer, The Procter & Gamble Company

I'm a big believer in simplicity, transparency, and fundamentals. My advice to an investor is to look for companies that are pretty easy to understand and that focus on long-term growth and leadership. Ask a few basic questions before deciding to invest:

Can they explain their business model or strategy in a single sentence?

Do they have clear goals and strategies that don't change from year to year?

Do they stay close to the consumers or customers they serve?

Do they have long-standing relationships with the leading supply and distribution partners in their industry?

Do they have a track record for setting the pace of innovation, executing with excellence, managing cash and costs for long-term growth, and delivering on the commitments they make to investors?

Do they develop leaders for the long term?

These are simple questions, but there are never enough companies that do all these things well over time. Concentrate on these basics, and you'll find companies worth considering for your investment dollars.

ALEXANDRA LEBENTHAL

President, Lebenthal & Co.

In my family, investment advice was always out there—it was part of the dinner conversation and part of our daily lives. My family made sure I was educated about financial information and financial products. My dad has done such an amazing job over the years of speaking in plain English about what investing is all about and educating people about it. That is something I ended up inheriting. My grandmother was also very focused on making sure investors weren't just relying on us to tell them what to do. She wanted them to understand it for themselves.

When clients said, "Well if you say it's okay, then I guess go ahead and do it," my grandmother would say, "No, you must understand this yourself, I am going to make you do the arithmetic." She would make them get a pencil and paper and she would teach them how to understand their finances. She was full of statements like "don't live beyond your means," which is something that I've tried to follow (though not always successfully!), and I've passed that knowledge on to other people as well. For example, don't get into credit card debt. If you do, you are giving up the opportunity to invest your own money because you owe money. Another thing my grandmother stressed was making sure we knew how to properly endorse a check. To this day I still write *for deposit only*. I never just sign my name.

There is so much publicity and information about certain parts of the market like mutual funds and stocks that other areas like the bond market seem to be shrouded in mystery. People tend to be less invested because they don't know where to get the information. I don't know everything my doctor knows, and I shouldn't be expected to. He or she needs to teach me. The same applies to investing. People think they should know it all and they are afraid to ask the questions, but in fact people in the financial business love answering questions and being able to teach people. People need to feel more comfortable with this whole education aspect. If they are dealing with someone who doesn't want to provide that, then they should find another financial expert. Unfortunately, over the years financial advisors, brokers, and salespeople have gotten a bad rap but in reality we are great resources for people who want information and an education so don't be afraid to use us.

Once you have educated yourself, diversity in a portfolio is the most important thing. You should never have all your eggs in one basket. Time and time again markets and different asset classes have shown us that things are going to perform differently so it's vital that you take the time to understand everything that's out there.

It's important to have something in your portfolio that isn't "big money." Bonds are the stable part of your portfolio, they are what you can depend on, the thing you can plan on. Also, they provide income and if you don't need the income you can use it to reinvest in other bonds or stocks. Having that steady stream of income is a gift.

I really care about people doing the right thing and feeling comfortable and feeling they have someone who works with them, who respects them, who wants to teach them, who wants to be an advisor and a part of their financial life, as well as the rest of their life. Too often we assume that if you're in the money business, there shouldn't be a human element but there absolutely should be. To me the two are inseparable.

JOE LEE

Chairman, Darden Restaurants, Inc.

There are two people who gave me great advice early in my life. One was my dad and the other was my grandfather. They had similar messages. My father taught me the importance of saving early and saving often, which translates into investing early and investing often. Start early, have a plan, and stay with it. My grandfather told me to be sure you know what you're investing in because there are a lot of people who want to sell you anything. It's up to you to educate yourself about potential investments. You have to do the homework and there's never been a time when that advice is more valuable than today.

Ideally, our school systems would start to teach students how to manage money when they are in grammar school. There is such an absence of knowledge in how money works and how to

grow investments. Unfortunately, most people
have to learn the way I did—through the school
of hard knocks.

Start investing as early as you can and invest
for your life cycle. Some people should invest
with more speculation, while others should invest with more security and guaranteed interest.
Figure out what stage of life you are in and invest accordingly. Be a long-term investor. Unless
you are a professional trader, don't try to time
the market. It is highly unlikely you will do well.
Numerous studies have shown that even professional traders do not do as well as those who are
investing in the long term. When you look at a
company you should ask, "Does this company
have good leadership? Does this company provide a product or service that is greatly desired
or needed by people? Do they have a long-term
market?"

If you find a company with good leadership,
invest early. Don't try to overtrade the company.
The expenses of turning over the stock will wind
up taking profits out of your pocket. Stay with
the investment and understand the industry.
Don't just invest once and assume that everything will go well. You need to know if something is suddenly happening to the company or
industry that would cause you to have to sell it.

You need to have appropriate diversity in
your portfolio. Adequate diversification comes

quicker than you expect. In other words, you don't need to have 100 stocks if you are careful and are investing in quality companies in an industry and you are diversifying the number of industries you are in. It doesn't take much more than one or two dozen stocks to give you a very good diversification portfolio. If you are invested in 100 different stocks, you have too many companies and industries on your plate and it will be impossible to adequately stay current with them. This is when you can run into trouble and miss something important.

STEVE LEUTHOLD

Founder and Chairman,
Leuthold Weeden Capital Management

On my path of learning about the investment world, the most enlightening experience I had was my six years as a retail stockbroker. In the early 1960s, I was working at Paine Webber and I learned some very important lessons.

Hardly anyone ever makes money from short-term trading. We're all too emotional about things. In the investment world, sticking to your set disciplines is absolutely essential. You've got to set them up and stay true to them.

Back in the 1960s, I started developing a process where we looked at a series of different indicators and then looked at the net result. Since then, we've added to this equation and it has grown to 170 different factors today. It is essential for our company to use disciplines like this because it allows us to be aggressive. In

1970, I bought stocks as the market bottomed and emotionally I thought, *This has got to be wrong. I know it's got to be wrong. We're getting bankruptcies, we're getting all these things falling down around us, what are we doing?* This is the most important time to trust in your disciplines.

The key philosophy I've developed over the years is *not to lose.* We always look at odds and indicators and we're never fully invested—we never go more than 70 percent in common stock. I've also learned that cash is not trash. If you don't have cash available, you can't take advantage of opportunities. Cash gives you the availability to step in there when there are opportunities to develop. Cash is a very valuable offensive weapon. For individuals, the one thing that people should do is look for mutual funds or money managers that are balanced and flexible instead of people who play all-out 100 percent equities all the time.

We are all subject to the herd psychology, so it can be difficult to stick to your disciplines. When you go to a cocktail party and everyone is making money by buying a second home or a third home or they are leveraging their home and buying four condos, it is difficult to stand against that. The key is to keep some kind of a constant ratio between your equities and equity alternatives and readjust that every year. For example, say you want to have 20 percent invested in the stock market. At the end of the year, you are up 23 percent. *Take 3 percent off the table.* If you have a good gain, take some of it and put it away or move it to another area you are underweight in. If people would do that and ignore the chatter at cocktail parties, they would be much better off. Do your best to avoid being inundated with headlines and newspapers and television information. The wisest thing is to set a ratio and once a year reexamine it and change it around.

Don't get greedy. I've always told people if you want to try to shoot the moon, take 5 or 10 percent for your play money and run it yourself. You're not risking too much of your net worth so you can be greedy and have some fun with it. But take the bulk of your money and put it into a sensible fixed ratio program that you reevaluate annually. Take some kind of an unbreakable vow that you won't touch it during the interim period.

EDWARD J. LUDWIG

**Chairman, President, and
Chief Executive Officer,
Becton, Dickinson and Company**

The best investment advice I ever heard was from Peter Lynch, the famed manager of the Fidelity Magellan Fund whose video we used at Becton, Dickinson and Company to educate our associates. He said, "Don't invest in anything you don't understand." This could also be interpreted as "Only invest in those things that you do understand."

Other good advice I received years ago was to invest and save, even in small amounts, but with every paycheck. The critical point is to start young, start early, and commit to it. Doing it at all is smarter than doing nothing.

Ultimately, I combined these two ideas and I have made three principal types of investments so far in my life:

I have invested in my company's (BD) stock.
I have invested in my sons' education.
I have invested in two quality residences, for
day-to-day living and vacations.

All of these investments have yielded excellent
returns—in the financial, psychological, and
lifestyle areas. I am now diversifying into high-
quality, laddered fixed income securities to balance my portfolio.

TERRY LUNDGREN

Chairman, President, and Chief Executive Officer, Federated Department Stores, Inc.

Follow the path of your own experience.

Your years of experience coupled with your instincts are the best guide for your business and personal investment decisions.

Follow them.

HOWARD LUTNICK

**Chief Executive Officer,
Cantor Fitzgerald**

Since I had lost both parents when I was young,
I was responsible for my financial future. During
my freshman year at Haverford College, a
friend of mine took me to see a couple of
people he knew to get some investment advice.
One of them was Bernie Cantor. He gave me
safe advice: Take no risk. Given who you are,
an eighteen-year-old, you need the money to
live. Put your money in U.S. Treasuries so you
cannot lose the principal. A fundamental rule of
investing is that your perspective will change
depending on where you are in life. This is
classic life-cycle investing. While you are
earning money and capable of paying for your
family's needs, additional money beyond that
can be available for riskier investing. But if you

are not able to pay your rent and you are not living the lifestyle you want to live, then your money can't be put at risk. It needs to be protected so that you can live the best you can within your circumstances.

Stock tips are a bad idea. My advice is never take a stock tip from someone who doesn't come to work in a limousine. I am not in favor of buying single stocks because I think it is impossible to have enough information to do it successfully. Most people look at their stocks like they look at a marriage. They buy 100 shares of stock, and they will tell you a story about it. "You know, back when I bought that stock, things were really good. I paid 10, then it was 12, then 14—the honeymoon was great—then it sort of got a little boring but I stuck it out. Then things got rough for a while. And now it's 6. But I've married this stock for better or worse, until death do we part so I'm hanging in there." Don't look at stocks like a marriage. When you buy a stock, you are just supposed to date it, sell it when it's up, and whatever you do, don't marry it.

KLAUS MARTINI

**Global Chief Investment Officer,
Deutsche Bank Private Wealth Management**

In the late 1970s, I was attending university in Munich and I spent quite a lot of time at the Munich stock exchange. There was a glass cage where visitors could sit and watch the investing scene. It was actually very boring, but every now and then you could pick up some good advice from the speculators who were there. These guys were really trying to play the insiders' scoops, which usually just ended up being rumors. At that time, you didn't have Reuters or Bloomberg so newspapers were the main source.

During university, I started investing in my first stocks. If I was standing close enough, I was able to pick up tips I'd overhear at the stock exchange. Rumors more than valuable tips, they nonetheless helped me out enough to make financing my studies a bit more bearable. Lis-

tening to the rumors and seeing how people re-
acted to the rumors was important. I was always
a momentum player. I didn't try to identify the
real value of stocks; instead, I jumped on the
bandwagon as early as possible. When you combine fundamental research with rumors, the
market becomes momentum-driven and emotion
begins to play an integral role.

For eighteen years, I was a portfolio manager.
Now I deal with private clients and I am faced
with an emotionally driven market every day. I
brought a lot of new commodities to our private
clients, but explaining the value of the commodities and why they should buy them takes
some time. Graphs and bar charts do not work.
I need to explain it in a way that is emotionally
connected to them. For example, to convince
people that gold is a great proposition I borrowed a visual technique from a former boss. I
ask my clients whether you could put all of the
gold in the world under the first arch of the
Eiffel Tower. It doesn't even come close. Gold is
a finite commodity and it would barely reach
halfway up the first arch. This story reaches my
clients on a basis that charts and graphs do not.
It takes the concept from an abstract level to a
level that they can grasp.

In investing, the most challenging thing is to
keep your emotions out of it. In the mid-1990s,
I made a mistake when I sold a 7 percent stake

in Nokia. I always look back and think, the stock moves so fast and I missed it completely. But you have to remind yourself that you are not alone in the market. There are a lot of people who are driven by emotions. And emotion is not always a negative thing. It can sometimes play a large role in the stock's story.

When you invest in a stock, it is important to know the full story of the stock. You should not get rid of the stock before the story is over. If you find a stock interesting, ride the bull until it breaks down. It usually takes much longer than you think for everybody to understand the story and by the end it is fraught with far more emotion than rational thinking.

There is an Austrian company called Wolford whose story perfectly illustrates the importance of emotion in relation to stock price. Wolford specializes in high-quality bodywear and swimwear. Founded in 1949, it came to the market in 1995. The company's goal was to brand itself as high-end retail. They launched a great campaign and published a hugely popular yearly calendar. Finally, it came to the market and the stock dropped. So, Wolford went on a public relations mission. Luxurious fashion shows in Rome on the Spanish Steps and high-profile relationships with all the large couture houses. Soon, the company began to gain some momentum and the stock started to go up. More and more people were buying into the "Wolford story" and the stock just kept rising. Nobody could believe it, but it did. In fact, the stock went up sevenfold over the next two years. But none of this was rational. It was simply an unstoppable (at the time) momentum driven by emotions. However, it is worth noting that today it is trading at its original 1995 trading price.

MACKEY J. MCDONALD

Chairman, President, and Chief Executive Officer, VF Corporation

The best investment advice I have ever received and adopted was a belief in and a commitment to my own company, VF Corp. This has proven to be particularly valuable as I acquired stock options and held on to them while the company built appealing lifestyle brands that created a connection with consumers. I'm still acquiring those options and watching them grow in value.

Since 1983, when I began as an assistant vice president with our Lee jeans division, I saw plenty to convince me of the long-term potential of VF stock because I saw personally the vision, work ethic, and professionalism of the people of VF.

There are few more satisfying business developments than creating a vision for growth and transforming the company to achieve that growth. VF has evolved from a basic apparel maker to a company driven by lifestyle brands that hold special appeal with consumers.

And during this period, our stock has risen from below $30 in 1996 to above $60 in 2005. We've certainly faced many challenges during that period, but the VF vision has carried us forward.

Of course, as a knowledgeable investor, I encourage everyone to diversify your portfolio, invite annual reviews by a professional advisor, and make important adjustments as your age, time horizon, and risk tolerance change.

ROGER MCNAMEE

**Co-founder and General Partner,
Integral Capital Partners**

My first boss said to me, "Roger, the first job of any investor is to know yourself." Beyond basic issues like risk profile, you also have to understand whether you are the kind of person who is genuinely interested in investing, someone who will do the research because it is fun and intellectually stimulating, or you are the kind of person who would love to get investment returns with a minimum of effort. You also need to know how you react to certain kinds of information. You need to take an honest look at your risk profile, commitment, and emotional tendencies.

The investment business rewards people who can think clearly and make decisions during times of change when the environment is foggy. If you're the kind of person who places emphasis on the most recent data point, you are less likely to be as successful as someone who can see the latest data point in the context of many years' worth of information. Knowing yourself is absolutely paramount. If you're the kind of person who doesn't need to look at the stock quote every day, then that's important to know. If you're the kind of person who loves to do research, who loves to spend time in the market, then making your own investment decisions is a great idea. If you're the kind of person who wants to get the returns but doesn't want to put a lot of time into it or you're the kind of person who cannot react dispassionately to changes, then you should certainly find someone else to manage your money.

A second important piece of advice is that you can generally lose more money in a matter of minutes than you can make in a matter of years. The lesson here is that avoiding losers is every bit as important as finding winners. When the market adjusts to bad news, it does so instantaneously, but when it adjusts to good news it tends to do so over a period of time and you get rewarded solely for your good ideas and punished for your bad ones. It has been my experience that the pursuit of a quick return is generally unproductive because people often want to buy a stock that has already gone up a lot so they tend to invest in things with an unfavorable risk reward.

A third piece of advice is that you should view the long term as a consistently infinite series of short terms. You cannot be successful in the long run without being successful most of the time in the short run. It is amazing to me how often people justify bad decisions with the notion that they are in it for the long haul. In fact, my first partner in Integral, John Powell, had a brilliant line. He said he learned in the retail brokerage business that most people's greatest comfort comes from stock positions that are a little bit underwater because they don't have to make a decision. Once the stock is in the money, they are worried that they need to sell it, and if they lose a lot of money they know they need to sell it, but if they are just losing a little bit of money, they sleep fine. That is not a great situation. I am a believer in having a very long-term investment plan. I am a believer in dollar cost averaging, which basically says if you make the decision to buy a security—any stock or bond—you decide how much your total commitment is going to be and then you make the investment in tranches of equal size over a period of time. If you are investing $10,000, you might invest in ten chunks of $1,000 or five chunks of $2,000 spread over a predetermined period. This approach protects you from wild fluctuations.

I am a believer that the really important trends in any sector, including my core sector of technology, tend to last a decade or more. You don't need to be in a rush. In fact, being in a rush causes you to make mistakes far more often than it rewards you. In 1987 when the market crashed, there weren't a lot of lessons to be learned because it affected every stock equally. In the summer of 1990, we had another period when stocks went down a lot but it wasn't uniform. At that time, I owned three stocks when I was managing the fund at T. Rowe Price. Those stocks taught me some serious lessons. In particular, I learned the brutal lesson that you can lose more money in seconds than you can make in years. We were one of Oracle's largest shareholders. Oracle had gone public in 1986 and it had been growing 100 percent or more in every single report. They were really fixated on it. You could see that the balance sheet was deteriorating, the income statement was deteriorating and they were making the 100 percent with smoke and mirrors. But I just couldn't bear the thought of missing the last 10 percent on the upside. As a consequence, even though I had all the information, I overstayed my welcome.

What I have learned is that by being a very detailed analyst as well as a portfolio manager, the mistakes I make are seldom due to my not having the right piece of information. It is usually because I didn't place the appropriate weight on the information that mattered. Today we are in a position where the Internet, Reg FD, and the Sarbanes-Oxley Act all work to level the playing field for everyone and there is seldom an excuse for not having the information necessary to make a good investment decision. The challenge is to place it in the proper context. If you discover that stocks are moving for reasons you did not anticipate, you should ask yourself whether you are working hard enough. You are competing against people who do it for a living and for whom investing is not just a career, but a passion. If you are willing to put the time into your research, you can eliminate many, if not most, of the advantages that professional investors once had.

ALAN B. MILLER

Founder, Universal Health Services, Inc.

Growing a company that is a solid investment for others and raising capital many times showed me how to be a good investor. As my company, Universal Health Services, developed, our investors demonstrated their confidence in us. I learned that they followed the company because of me and the team I assembled and our track record. Invest with competent successful management, that's the key. It is the same in all business—it's the management!

JOE MOGLIA

Chief Executive Officer, TD Ameritrade

The first time I thought about investing was when I was nine years old. Neither one of my parents had a high school education and my father owned a fruit and vegetable store that I worked at on Saturdays during the summer. I was always aware of the fact that seven of us—I was the oldest of five—lived in a two-bedroom, one-bathroom apartment in Manhattan. We always had enough to eat and we never felt that we didn't have money, but my friends went on vacations and we never did things like that. From a monetary perspective, when you are a kid you look at investing in terms of what it can do for you.

I remember asking my father why we didn't take vacations. He explained to me that the store required a lot of hours, a lot of responsibility, and that you had to be there in order to have the opportunity to save your money. I asked, "Well, what do you do when you save your money?" That was when he told me about the stock market. So, my introduction to investing didn't come about because my dad was some big Wall Street investor; it was because I was wondering why we never went on vacation.

My father read the newspapers for financial information, but his reading choice was usually *The Daily News*. He definitely wasn't poring over research reports at the end of the day after working a fourteen-hour shift at the store. Sometimes a Wall Street guy would swing by the store to pick up some groceries on his way home and my father would overhear him talking about the stocks he bought that day. My father acted like this was virtually insider information and he immediately bought the stock.

But he was an extremely safe investor. If GM was trading at 10, once it got to 11 or 12, he was out! And he was very happy to make $100 or $200 without having to work. Sometimes things didn't go so well and he didn't sell early enough. I remember his talking to me about Penn Central when he bought it at 10, then it went down to 5, then 3, then eventually went bankrupt. What I learned from my father is that it would probably make sense to do a little homework and to have a reason other than somebody else told you to buy it. Incorporate a strategy into your investing. For example, if you own it at a certain price, determine when and why you should sell. When I was a kid watching my father, I learned to never emotionally tie yourself to an investment because that is when it is difficult to make the right decisions. As I got more involved in Wall Street, I kept going back to the fundamentals: not being emotionally involved, having a disciplined strategy, having an objective and goal, understanding what that is, and implementing a plan that you adhere to for the majority of the time but you aren't tied to.

As I moved into the executive management ranks at Merrill Lynch and began to receive stocks, my mentors told me, "If you believe in what we are doing and you're a part of it, you don't want to sell your stock." I looked at so many other people who would turn around and sell their stocks. The most significant part of my net worth before going to Ameritrade was the fact that I had never sold a share of Merrill Lynch until four years ago. That accumulation over time was a big deal. If you're part of an organization that you believe in and you're contributing to it, don't be afraid to put too many eggs into a basket that you have some influence over.

There are a few mistakes that people make over and over again. First, they are too emotionally tied to the investments. Second, they think too much about the basis of the price at which they bought a particular security. Where they bought it is irrelevant. They need to focus on where it is ultimately going to go. Third, we all recognize how important it is to have some sort of reasonable semblance of financial well-being for your future, your children's education, whatever is important to you, but so few people take real responsibility for that. Unfortunately, Wall Street goes out of its way to make investing, especially portfolio investing, incredibly sophisticated and complex because they can make a tremendous amount of money by doing so. It's not in their best interest to simplify this process, but the fact of the matter is that it is not that difficult. Most families will spend more time trying to research where their next vacation is going to be than they will researching and taking responsibility for what they're trying to do from an investment perspective.

To be a successful investor, you need to have a thorough understanding, both intellectually and emotionally, of what your risk tolerance is. There are plenty of people who intellectually understand *I can afford to lose $10,000*, but emotionally they may not be able to handle that. As a stock goes up and down, they can't sleep at night. It is important to develop a risk profile that helps you understand where and how you might want to invest. Then you have to understand what diversification is and how important it is to diversify. These are concepts that aren't complex. All investors should be able to understand and implement them.

GEORGETTE MOSBACHER

**Chief Executive Officer,
Borghese Cosmetics**

The best investment advice I've ever received is: "There's no such thing as a dumb question when it comes to your own money."

You have to take ownership of your finances! Even though it's your money, we often abdicate that responsibility to others.

This is particularly true of women. Traditionally, we thought that the men in our lives would "take care of us." The fallacy of that belief struck home in my own family. My father was killed in an auto accident when my mother, a typical homemaker, was twenty-seven years old and left with four young children to raise. In addition to the trauma, she didn't have a clue whether my dad had life insurance, what our mortgage payments were, even if the car itself was paid for.

Men will often turn over all their money to professional advisors (in "blind trust," if you will). They should be asking questions regardless of how silly or stupid the question may seem to be. All aspects of our investments should be compatible with your personal comfort level and your instincts.

Because there is an emotional component to your financial decisions, you have to be tuned in both emotionally and intellectually. Question yourself as well. How do *you* feel about what is being proposed? Or, executed? I believe that you simply can't ask enough questions! It's all about your own well-being . . . and often your very survival.

Today, it's much easier to be well informed. If you are not getting the quality of information you need to make informed decisions, you have the Internet and a myriad of publications to help. You can ask for written information from your advisors and certainly get everything in writing. You've got to read everything! Highlight what you don't understand and don't be embarrassed to ask for written answers. Keep the most important financial information in a safe place. Don't put reading aside, thinking: "I'll get to this when I have time." You know very well that there might never be time.

Remember, the "Buck Stops with You!" The more you ask, the more you'll know and the safer and more secure you'll be!

Angelo Mozilo

Co-founder and Chief Executive Officer,
Countrywide Financial Corporation

About twenty years ago while playing a round of golf with a close friend of mine who was a seasoned investor, I asked him what his approach was toward his investing disciplines. At this time, I had little to show for my investing efforts and with five children I felt it was important to have a more intelligent and disciplined approach to my investment style. His advice was as follows:

Investments should be broken into *three* specific and well-defined buckets.

The first bucket is for money that will be absolutely safe no matter what happens in the world. It's a bucket that assures that irrespective of external circumstances you and your family will be financially secure. This bucket contains

Treasuries, agencies, and triple A insureds. This should be your largest bucket.

The second bucket contains equities of world-class companies possessing a superior long-term track record, a relevant product or service, and a time-tested business plan. There must be a long-term commitment to this bucket and it should be reviewed on a regular basis to determine if any fundamental changes have taken place thereby requiring a change in the mix. This bucket should be approximately 30 to 40 percent of your holdings.

The third bucket is known as the "go for the gusto" pot and would include junk bonds, high-risk stocks, and from time to time a trip to Las Vegas. You should be emotionally prepared to lose everything in this bucket but if you hit pay dirt the returns will be high. This pot should be less than 10 percent and preferably 5 percent of your holdings.

Being a CEO of a Fortune 200 company, I have the opportunity not only to observe what's going on within Countrywide but also to interact with CEOs from major corporations throughout the world. I am unconditionally convinced that the quality of any company is a direct result of the *quality of management and the people they manage.* If you have mediocre management, you will have a company with mediocre performance. There is no cure for mediocrity except to surgically extract it out of the organization, particularly out of the senior management level. Mediocre managers inevitably recruit mediocre people. It has, therefore, been my experience that investors must focus their attention and analysis on the *quality of leadership* in any organization that they are seeking as an investment opportunity. It is the people who create the business plan, who build the processes, who create the technology, who execute the tasks that deliver the product or service, and who determine the success or failure of a business. If you study companies that are selling the same product and/or service and one is successful and one is not, you can easily find the answer in the *leadership and the culture* that they create within the organization.

My shareholders have been the beneficiary of some insightful investment advice I received almost twenty-five years ago from my former partner, co-founder and co-author of the *Quality of Earnings Report* service, Thornton L. O'glove. *Quality of Earnings* inferentially analyzed corporate financial statements and footnotes and alerted institutional investors to early warning signs of potential earnings overstatements or understatements.

Before founding the research service, Thornton L. O'glove and I were research analysts at a small retail brokerage firm back in the late 1960s. At the time, I believed my job was to select winning stocks by extracting meaningful information from management. My reliance on management contact resulted in the first serious failure of my young life. A company I had recommended as a buy missed management's projections by a wide margin causing material losses for the firm's clients. I had bought into management projections without question. However, Mr. O'glove showed me that if I had paid attention to the early warning alerts on the firm's financial statements, which began to appear eighteen months before the disappointing results, I would never have believed management's projections.

He went on to provide me with the following insightful advice to which I attribute my success as a Wall Street money manager. Mr. O'glove told me that the stock market was a loser's game, a game in which you had to analyze your potential downside on investments before evaluating your upside potential. He went on to say that big losers hurt investment results by a far greater extent than big profits help. For example, an 80 percent up year followed by a 50 percent down year results in a 10 percent loss of capital, not a 30 percent gain.

If defense is the most important aspect of investing, then an investor must look at the potential negatives that could affect a company before considering the positive aspects. Speaking to management is not the best source for negative information, as management has a vested interest in putting its best foot forward. The only way to analyze a company and judge the quality of management is to look at what management *is doing* as portrayed in the financial statements rather than what they *are saying*.

As a result of Mr. O'glove's wisdom, I have spent my entire career looking behind the numbers of financial statements, identifying warning alerts indicative of unexpected changes in a company's earnings power, and this process has saved me from many errors, including Boston Chicken, Lucent, and Enron. I would rather spend one night with the financial statements than two days with management.

In order to profit in the stock market, an investor must purchase good companies, pay the right price, and anticipate future earnings power not currently priced into the stock. The ability to inferentially analyze financial statements and look for early warning alerts portending that current earnings expectations are either too pessimistic or optimistic should provide investors with a decided advantage in reaching their capital gains objectives. The ability to sell a stock when future expectations appear unrealistic based on an analysis of financial statements has been the most important factor that I can attribute to my investment success. Following crowds is usually dangerous to your investment health. Thank you, Ted O'glove.

JOHN MYERS

**President and Chief Executive Officer,
GE Asset Management**

I've had the good fortune to work with and learn from some of the best investors over the past twenty years. People like John Angelo, Lee Cooperman, Bill Grant, Ken Langone, Lionel Pincus, Art Samberg, and many others. All of them are smart, do their due diligence, and have great people supporting them on their investment teams.

I think the common characteristics that differentiate the best investors from so many other average performers is their ability to assess the risk versus reward, their ability to cut losses early when the game changes, and the confidence to go with their instincts. I was lucky to pay my "stupid tax" early enough in my career so that I learned more in experience than I lost in dollars. Let me cite an example in my career where these characteristics paid off for me.

I was running the GE Pension Fund real estate group in the late 1980s when we decided to invest in a small Northeastern U.S. hotel management company named Guest Quarters (GQ) together with a portfolio of five GQ-branded all-suite hotels. It proved to be the wrong time in the business cycle, and before long the company's senior debt was in default and I was heading to Pittsburgh, Pennsylvania, to negotiate with the senior lender, Westinghouse Credit (W).

I prepared myself with all the arguments I could think of to support W granting us concessions on a lower interest rate and extended maturities in exchange for a larger share of the future equity economics. W came to the meeting with a totally different objective. They wanted to be 100 percent bought out. I wasn't prepared to talk buyout and had no approval from my executive committee, but I sensed a strong eagerness from W to get an offer from me. In fact, I was encouraged to make an offer and told they wouldn't be "upset" no matter what it was. (As it later turned out, W had bigger problems in their overall portfolio and were looking to value and monetize some assets to get a true idea of what they were worth.)

The opening was apparently there so I decided to go for it and offered them $35 million for their $130 million face-value position backed by my personal commitment to have the cash in their bank account the next day. That was either stupid or gutsy depending on your point of view, since I hadn't fully analyzed the value for a buyout and had zero authority to make such an offer.

Contrary to the assertion that they wouldn't get upset, they did, but we kept talking and less than a week later we agreed on a price about a 65 percent discount from face and I was able to secure the necessary approvals to close the deal.

We then used our senior debt position, which we had just acquired, to consolidate our equity ownership position to 100 percent as the other equity partner declined to participate on the debt buyback. We then were lucky to recruit two experienced hotel industry pros, Peter Ueberroth and Dick Ferris, to invest with us as partners and manage the company as co-chairmen. The strategy was to grow the management platform, as we all thought the timing was right for a new player in the hotel industry to acquire other assets and consolidate.

We bought Doubletree Hotels from Canadian Pacific, bought Red Lion from KKR, took the company public through an IPO, and then merged with Promus hotels (Embassy Suites and Hampton Inns) and ultimately sold the whole company to Hilton Hotels, realizing about $400 million in gains. Peter Ueberroth and I went on the Hilton board of directors, we retained a significant amount of Hilton shares, and have since participated in a nice appreciation in the share price.

Sometimes if you've done a lot of analysis and believe strongly in a strategy but get the initial timing wrong, you need to step back and trust your instincts. The worst thing to do is to dwell on your mistake and do nothing. If the facts have changed or you're wrong, act quickly to accept it and get out of the investment. If you're convinced you're right, take the opportunity to strengthen your position and "go for the gold." No guts, no glory is a terrific sports metaphor but it can work in business as well . . . so long as you're right.

Marilyn Carlson Nelson

Chairman and Chief Executive Officer, Carlson Companies

No single piece of advice covers all situations in life, or investing. So my investment strategy is triangulated by much good advice given to me through the years.

The old Swedish maxim of "never row out farther than you can swim back" might at first seem strange advice coming from someone who once had bet all he had—no, make that all that he *didn't* have—to start a company near the end of the Depression. It was in 1938 that my fresh-out-of-school father, Curt Carlson, started Gold Bond Stamps on $55 he borrowed from his landlord. But as the years progressed, along with his success, I saw again and again how he would take big chances yet never jeopardize the "center" of our family's future. There was always a core upon which he could rebuild, even if his latest bet didn't pay off. Of course, he also believed that a successful entrepreneur is a person who reduces his risks as much as possible—so even his bets weren't always gambles.

A second good piece of investment advice came directly from my father and had to do with investments in philanthropy. He always believed that "the best philanthropy is a job," and directed his energies along the lines of business, rather than foundation work. But when he did practice philanthropy, he did so with typical verve and commitment—he and a small group of Minneapolis families formed the nation's first "Five Percent Club," committing 5 percent of pretax profits to community causes.

When my father began to endow programs and buildings in the Twin Cities, especially at the University of Minnesota, which had given him his education, he tended to put the Carlson name on the gifts and structures. Once while I was young and feeling particularly noble, I asked him if the more selfless approach might be to donate these gifts anonymously, without connection to the Carlson name.

The advice he gave me has stayed with me until this day. "Marilyn," he said, "by putting our family's name on something, I'm not just committing the funding—I'm committing the future support of you and your heirs. Every time you drive by that building, or participate in that program, I want you to feel an obligation to make sure it is as good as it can be, because it carries your name." Talk about a gift that keeps on giving!

The third piece of good investment advice I received wasn't investment advice at all when it was offered, but it has become such for me since.

During the 1980s, while our country was still sorting out the social changes of the 1960s and 1970s, I served on the board of Northwestern Bell, one of the baby Bells then going through the difficulties of the AT&T breakup. A man named Jack MacAllister was the head of that particular Bell division, and one day he brought a problem to the board. He reported that many of the women and minorities who had progressed into Bell management were being deployed to head operations across Northwestern Bell's seven-state area, but not being accepted into the various social and civic organizations in their towns because of their gender or race.

Jack told the board, "We're going to pull Northwestern Bell support from all these organizations, because we cannot support them yet let them turn away our managers." The board balked, and cautioned him against picking a fight with these powerful local groups in the midst of the AT&T breakup struggles. The consensus of the board was that "it's a good idea, but this is not the time." To this, Jack replied, "Oh? When is the time?"

Just how is this investment advice?

Today's corporations and investors have never-before-seen power and influence. With this new power has come new responsibility. Yet too many make the long view unacceptable, by buying and selling based solely on quarterly returns.

Investors can make a difference, by making capital available to the formerly disenfranchised . . . by supporting expansion of entrepreneurial opportunities to women and minorities and developing nations . . . by investing in socially responsible companies. By using their influence, investors can require management of their companies to answer that question posed by Jack MacAllister more than two decades ago: If this is not the time for positive change, then when *is* the time?

BILL NYGREN

Portfolio Manager, The Oakmark Funds

The best investment advice I ever received was from Benjamin Graham in his book *The Intelligent Investor*. His was the first investment book I read that approached buying and selling stocks with the same thought process one would use for buying and selling businesses. His wonderful parable, "Mr. Market," made the common sense of value investing jump out at me. In that parable, Graham supposed that you purchased a small part of a business for $1,000 and that your overly emotional partner, Mr. Market, offered daily to buy or sell an interest in that same business for extremely high or low prices that were based on his mood rather than on business developments. Of course Graham went on to equate Mr. Market with the daily price swings in the stock market and concluded that a rational investor could exploit a market that occasionally gets swept up in the emotions of fear and greed.

Our approach to stock selection for The Oakmark Funds takes advantage of Mr. Market's emotional swings. We attempt to identify good businesses that are being managed to benefit their shareholders, and purchase them only when investors' negative emotions have created the opportunity to acquire shares at well below intrinsic value. We then wait patiently for a mood swing that results in the stock price increasing to its intrinsic value. That may happen quickly or, more likely, may occur over multiple years. When price and value do ultimately converge, we sell and start the process over again with a different stock. By utilizing a business value approach to selecting stocks, our process focuses on business characteristics such as earnings, cash flow, return on investment, market share, and industry growth. We can ignore the day-to-day flow of news, economic statistics, market swings, and so on that often takes investor attention away from what really matters—the value of the ownership interest in a business that their stock certificate represents.

ROBERT A. OLSTEIN

**Chairman, Chief Executive Officer, and
Chief Investment Officer,
Olstein & Associates**

Lucky Eleven Top Investment Tips:

1. Attempts to predict movements of the stock market in order to profit therefrom is a long-term-failure process.

   Market risk can be controlled somewhat by allocating your portfolio between riskless fixed income securities and equities, rather than diversifying your portfolio according to artificial investment barriers such as large-cap, small-cap, growth, value, and so on.

2. Accurate economic forecasts are largely unnecessary.

   Interest rates and future cash flow (as opposed to reported earnings) are the only important economic variables to consider when valuing a stock.

3. Current news is of little help in managing your money.

   The market looks to the future and money is made when investors spot or identify deviations between short-term perceptions and longer-term reality.

4. The three most important characteristics to consider when selecting a stock are price, price, price.

   Paying the wrong price for a good company is the equivalent of buying a bad company.

5. Investment managers making the fewest errors are usually the best long-term performers.

   Thus, consider downside risk when purchasing a security before considering upside potential.

6. The best way to protect against financial risk is to buy companies that generate excess cash flow (more cash coming in than going out after capital expenditures and working capital needs) at a discount to intrinsic value (defined as the present value of future excess cash flow).

   Excess cash flow companies can raise the dividend, buy back stock, make acquisitions when others may not, do not have to adopt short-term strategies that are not in the long-term interest of the company when problems develop, and are also good acquisition candidates.

7. The most important virtue of a value investor is patience.

Periods of misperception or negativity, which produce discount prices, may take considerable time to unwind. However, the rewards when and if the misperception is corrected can produce favorable investment results.

8. The desire to be right *all of the time* is a roadblock to being right *over time.*

Waiting for a catalyst to appear before buying an undervalued stock will usually result in the purchase of a fully valued stock. The timing in value investing is paying the right price.

9. Setting up artificial barriers to investing can limit performance.

The search for value cannot be limited. Value can occur in large companies, small companies, cyclical companies, growth companies, technology companies, etc.

10. A value investor needs to have a strict sell discipline that reaches conclusions based on excess cash flow valuations rather than price momentum or crowd psychology.

Tax implications of stock sales must take

a backseat to overvaluation, or you may never have any taxes to pay.

11. Even the best managers go through periods of under-performance.

Pick managers who have an investment discipline you can relate to and do not get involved in short-term performance or relative performance measures. Long-term (three to five years or more) absolute performance is the ultimate measure of investment success.

Suze Orman

**Best-selling Author and
Personal Finance Expert**

When I was about twelve years old, my family was not doing very well, financially speaking. I never quite got it, because at this time my dad had a little 400-square-foot deli. I used to work there, and I remember that people would line up out the door and he was busy all the time. But we still never had any money and I never quite understood why. One weekend I went to downtown Chicago with all my friends and we went to a deli. The sandwiches were half the size as my dad's and they were at least two to three times more expensive than my father's. I thought, *Wow, I have the key to my family's future.*

When I got back home, I said, "Dad, I know how we can become rich." He said, "Okay, let me hear it." I said, "You just have to double or triple the price of your sandwiches." He looked at me and said, "Suze, I'd much rather have 50 percent of something than 100 percent of nothing." I looked at him and said, "Um, all right." But I understood what he was telling me.

In 1998 and 1999, I made purchases in the technology area that I made a fortune on. I watched Safeguard Scientific quadruple from where I bought it. Some stocks were up 1,000 percent from where I purchased them. In 2000, the markets started to go down little by little. Everybody was saying, "Don't worry, it's going to turn around, it's going to come back, there's a lot more money to be made here." But I kept hearing my father's voice, *It's better to have 50 percent of something than 100 percent of nothing.* And I sold everything.

When you watch television every day and the majority of people are saying, "It's going to go up, this is a temporary pull-back, don't worry about it," and the gains had been extraordinary, 2001 hadn't happened yet, and the thought of not making as much as you could have is almost worse than when you buy something and lose money. When you buy something and it goes up and you sell it and then it goes up another 50, 100, 200 percent, you are so upset because the entire time you are calculating in your mind what you *could have had.*

But what you could have had is a dream. It's not life. That's why selling is so hard. When a stock goes down you don't want to sell it because of fear and hope—you're afraid it's going to go back up and you hope that it's going to.

It's better to have 50 percent of something than 100 percent of nothing always pops into my head and I make sure I listen to it. I sold 100 percent—lock, stock, and barrel. I kept my gains and I took everything I had and put it into the municipal bond market as I proceeded to watch the markets go down and down and down. I watched Safeguard Scientific go all the way down to a dollar a share. I watched every stock that I had sold go down the tubes to essentially nothing and I watched fortunes turn into dust. I watched joy turn into tears. I watched retirement plans go out the window and turn into twenty more years of working. I watched homes that had been leveraged lost because people went on margin. These people ended up with 100 percent of nothing.

The biggest mistake people make in investing is they get greedy. You can always buy back into something but you can't always sell when there's nothing left to sell. You can always buy back in if you are wrong. You cannot sell when it has turned to dust. It is over. Buying is easy. Selling is absolutely the most difficult thing to do. Fear, shame, and anger are the three internal obstacles to wealth. People who are ruled by emotions make emotional decisions when it comes to their money.

The majority of financial people that everyday people listen to are nothing more than salespeople. They are not the ones picking the stocks, they are not the ones making the decisions in the mutual funds—they are simply there to sell you the research or advice of the financial advisors and analysts that the brokerage firms have employed. They are ruled by emotions and they need to make as much money as you need to make. They need to compete with people in their field as much as you need to compete with people in your field. They need to have incentives put in front of them to do things they don't want to do, which the brokerage industries are very good at doing. The problem is that the individual investor is dealing with a middleman known as a "financial advisor" or "broker" who is ruled by emotions and is no more capable of making those decisions than you are.

The real financial whizzes are the ones who run the mutual funds, the ones who are the analysts but have absolutely no contact with the people who are investing the money. This enables the analyst to be very rational with their

thought process when the salesperson cannot.
Once a purchase is made, it is the emotional
salesperson who determines whether we sell or
keep holding on. And sometimes that person no
longer has access to the analyst. The analysts
are dealing with this on a technical level and
don't have to deal on an emotional level with
all the clients who have bought the mutual
fund.

So, why not just do it on your own, get rid
of the middleman and not deal with commissions since you're going to end up making the
same decisions no matter what? Why pay 5 percent to buy a mutual fund when you can buy a
no-load mutual fund on your own and probably come up with better results since you
didn't have to start 5 percent in the hole to
begin with?

Trust yourself more than you trust others. If
you walk into a financial advisor's office and
something doesn't feel right, do not talk yourself into it. In the long run, if you want the best
financial advisor in the world, you need to look
in the mirror. Nobody is going to care about
your money more than you do. These analysts
have to be accountable to their firm and there
is tremendous pressure on them. It takes a very,
very strong person not to succumb to pressure.

Start off by buying an index fund, get comfortable with dollar cost averaging, and practice diversification. Just see what it feels like to get your feet wet. We make it so complicated and it really is not.

JIM ROGERS

**JBR, International Investor,
and "Adventure Capitalist"**

Losing money is the best way to see what you're
made of. Remaining resilient once you lose
money teaches you about yourself and about the
market.

It's better to lose everything you've got when
it's only $5,000 rather than $5 million. Losing
money teaches you about yourself—can you
come back? Will you come back? Are you driven
enough to come back? Will you sell your motorcycle if you have to? If the first investment you
make turns out to be great, and then the next
four or five turn out great, you will think it is
easy and you will get sloppy and you won't appreciate how hard it can be, so if you get hit on
the head you won't be ready for it.

If you don't know what you're doing, don't
invest. If you are going to invest, only invest in

things you yourself know a lot about. I promise you that a newspaper or magazine is not going to teach you how to get rich. You're going to have to do a lot of hard work. Everyone reading this book knows a lot about something, whether it's fashion or cars, it's something. And that's what you should focus on—the things you already know a lot about, things that already interest you in your everyday life, and then expand on that and start reading the annual reports from those companies. Focus on what you're passionate about, then you'll figure out ways to make money on things you already know a great deal about and you won't have to rely on the magazines. Focus and follow your passion.

I'm always terrified every time I make an investment—I worry about everything all the time. I don't know what is going to come out of the blue and hit me. Who knows what's going to happen. If you're not worried, if you're not scared, then you're not much of an investor and you aren't doing a good job investing. You're getting sloppy and lazy.

WILBUR ROSS

**Billionaire, Internationally Acclaimed
"Turnaround Artist"**

When I first came to Wall Street, the treasurer of
Yale gave me some great advice. He had been the
advisor to my fraternity house so I got to know
him pretty well when I was president of my fraternity and he became sort of a mentor to me. He
had a couple of sayings that sound very folksy but
actually have an awful lot of logic to them.

One thing he said was that if something in an
investment opportunity seems too good to be
true, it probably *is* too good to be true. In fact,
there is probably something really wrong with it.
The second thing he told me is something I have
implemented throughout my career. He said
there is no proportionality between risk and reward. Think about it. For there to be a real proportionality, there would have to be some sort of
deity up in the sky saying, "Gee, you took a big

risk in that investment, therefore you get a big reward." But this investment deity does not exist. Whoever invented the saying that reward is proportional to risk was probably some Wall Street guy promoting a very risky deal. There is a relation between risk and reward but it is not as clear-cut as that saying. Frequently, you get paid for what people *perceive* to be the risk, but that may or may not at all correspond to the *actual* risk.

Throughout my career, I've taken the road less traveled. People thought there was no way there could be a steel industry that could make any profit at all in the United States. But the way we go about it, we make it profitable. First of all, we generally study an industry for a year or more before we actually make an investment in it. We spend a lot of time trying to figure out what would go bad and what the potential pitfalls will be. We've noticed that the companies in a given industry go bad more or less simultaneously. At one point in time, lots of retailers went bankrupt and then they got healthy. At another point in time, actually at several points in time, it was the airlines that all went bankrupt. At another point, it was the steel companies and at another it was the coal companies. Industries do go bad. Our job is to figure out whether there is one worth salvaging. But this process takes a great deal of patience and research.

What happens is that even professional investors have trouble controlling their own emotions. Inside every professional there lurks a regular person. They may have very good instincts, have done their research, and be on the verge of a great investment, but they get cold feet. Conventional wisdom and going with the herd outweigh having faith in their own beliefs. This is a mistake.

You need to avoid like the plague whatever is the most popular thing at the time. The biggest danger for the small investor is to get sucked up in whatever may be the flavor of the month. Don't get pulled into the market bubbles. If people would be a little more contrary in the decisions they make, they would be more likely to have investment success. For example, look for a well-known company, an established company, that for whatever reason is in a bad year. You are better off buying something like that and holding it than to choose the hot stock of the month. Choosing the latest hot stock is really just playing the game of "the last man out's the rotten egg." On the other hand, if you buy into an established company that isn't doing very well, there is a good chance the economy or industry will turn and you will make a profit off that investment.

The challenge in adhering to this type of investment philosophy is that most investors aren't willing to be disciplined enough. They aren't going to do the research on opportunities that aren't on the six o'clock news or found in the newspaper. Make an effort to add a little contrarianism to your portfolio. Generally, it is going against the grain that will better enable you to find investment success.

Tom Ryan

Chief Executive Officer,
CVS Corporation

The best advice I received was from my father. He said, "The only way to follow the stock market is to invest in a good management team and the only way to follow the horses is with a broom and a shovel."

RONALD L. SARGENT

Chairman and Chief Executive Officer, Staples, Inc.

Invest in yourself and your own capabilities. All too often, people invest in stocks and businesses they know little about and have no affinity for. As a result, they spend their time looking for the latest hot tip or sure thing, never having a true connection to their investments.

A wiser and more rewarding strategy is to invest in what you know and enjoy. You're more likely to understand the investments you're passionate about. The money does, in fact, follow.

For instance, I've never been passionate about office supplies in particular, but at the helm of Staples, I've been able to do things I do love, namely, build a great company, work with talented people, and find ways to make things work better.

Another example is a hobby. When I was a

kid, my father (a mechanic by trade and a man of modest means) bought and sold real estate. I guess the acorn didn't fall far from the tree, because I'm passionate about real estate as well. My hobby of renovating properties and then selling them feeds my creative side, and it's been lucrative as an investment strategy as well.

So, when you invest, make sure you know what you're investing in. Move toward opportunities you have an affinity and passion for. It will be a winning combination.

IRWIN SIMON

**Chief Executive Officer,
Hain Celestial Group, Inc.**

When I first recognized the business I wanted to invest in, two things were clear:

First, the health food industry would be a great opportunity to invest in and make a lot of money. There wasn't one particular individual doing it, but there were many people who were vying to supply healthy foods and, after watching people at a trade show, I realized there was a serious demand in that market. But nobody was adequately supplying it. Nobody was doing it correctly from a branding standpoint. Nobody was marketing it successfully. Second, changing the way the world eats was the inspiration for me. That is why the Hain Celestial Group was created.

During my days at Häagen-Dazs, I learned a valuable lesson that I have always stuck to.

People will always pay for brands. Reuben Mattus, the founder of Häagen-Dazs, taught me that people will pay for a good brand and they will pay for quality.

When I am investing my own money, I look for quality and I look for brands within a product. There are times when I second-guess myself. During the Internet bubble I thought, *Maybe I'm doing this wrong because the world is going to be inspired to grow through technology.* But in my business everything I do is tangible—you can touch it—it is very different from the tech world. There were times when I thought my formula was wrong, but thankfully I never changed my formula because the only things I would invest in today are brands that have a purpose. Unfortunately, some brands go out of style or are outdated so you need to ask, *What are the brands of tomorrow? What are the brands that are going to deliver quality?* If you go back twenty years, Whole Foods was not a place to shop. Today, Whole Foods is *the* place to shop.

Coca-Cola, a company with tremendous brand equity, is one of the number one brands in the world, but I am not sure that it is the brand for the next 100 years. What is in style? What is out of style? Today, Coca-Cola is an incredible brand, but take a step back and look at what people want. What will the next evolution of drinks be? Not soft drinks. From an investing standpoint you can say it is a great brand, but the more important question is *What will consumers want over the next 100 years?* How much more can Wal-Mart grow? What is the next Wal-Mart? That is what people should be looking to invest in because the world is not going to stand still. It is always changing.

ALAN SKRAINKA

Chief Market Strategist, Edward Jones

The best investment advice I ever received was from my mentor, Brad Perry, a brilliant investor and the former president and chairman of David L. Babson & Company. He taught me that the four most dangerous words in the world of investing are: "This time is different." He also taught me to be a realistic optimist, and to greet predictions from Wall Street, especially the long-term pessimistic ones, with a great deal of skepticism.

Here is how I would apply that advice to the current state of affairs:

I believe that not only is this time not different but that these are very normal times in which we live. In spite of a stock market that has moved sideways for five years, in spite of high oil prices, the conflict in Iraq, the War on Terrorism, concerns about Federal Reserve interest rate hikes, and other uncertainties, there is very little that is new, unusual, or different about the current state of affairs. It is not a time to be pessimistic regarding America's future.

Winston Churchill once said the further back you look, the further forward you can see. During World War II, many folks assumed that economic depression would be with us for a very long time. The belief was that the economy would slump back into depression as soon as the war was over, much like it did after World War I. The stock market took off after the Battle of Midway in 1942, which practically eliminated the threat of a Japanese invasion of California. The market continued to climb in anticipation of the postwar economic boom that would follow when the boys came home from the conflict overseas. Yet each time the economy entered recession, there were fears that it was just the beginning of another depression. In the meantime, inflation and unemployment remained remarkably low, much like they are today, and the stock market climbed the wall of worry.

In the 1960s, the Soviets threatened to "bury us" and the Cold War was in full swing. With the threat of nuclear missiles being planted just ninety miles from the Florida coast, schoolchildren practiced "duck and cover" drills in case of nuclear war. People in general just didn't feel very safe. By the mid-1960s, the ongoing prosperity convinced economists that the business cycle had been tamed by someone named John Maynard Keynes. Our President was convinced that a growing economy would provide enough revenue to greatly expand social programs at home, while fighting an unpopular war overseas.

The irrational exuberance of a long bull market came to an abrupt end with the United States held hostage by turmoil in the Middle East, and the Arab oil embargo in 1973. Economists proclaimed that the industrial West would forever be held hostage by Arab sheiks who controlled our future. A tripling of inflation followed, along with the President's resignation, a deep recession, and a wicked bear market the following year. President Ford felt that everyone should wear WIN buttons. "WIN" stood for "Whip Inflation Now." President Carter spoke of a "general malaise" that had gripped the country.

While the 1970s were difficult times for the financial markets, investors who continued to invest systematically, who focused on building portfolios that were balanced among domestic stocks, bonds, and foreign shares, and purchased high-quality common stocks that paid attractive dividends, generally held their own, and were well positioned for the great bull market that began in 1982.

The 1980s and 1990s were certainly not free of domestic problems, economic challenges, geopolitical conflict, or financial turbulence. For much of the 1980s, the United States spent enormous sums on defense in an effort to win the Cold War. The increase in spending, combined with large tax cuts, led to massive federal budget deficits. Economists said the federal government would crowd out the ability of corporations to borrow money and predicted skyrocketing interest rates. They also worried about the lack of competitiveness of American industry, which led many to buy books describing the Japanese style of management and quality control methods. The record one-day stock market crash in October 1987 convinced economists that a deep decline in the U.S. economy would soon follow.

In the early 1990s, with the Dow hovering around 3,000, investors worried about the first President Bush's reelection, conflict in Iraq, high oil prices, and a weak economy. We got out of Iraq, Bush lost the election, oil prices came down, and the economy prospered. The decade of the 1990s ended with more irrational exuberance, with investors believing that the Internet had spawned a "new economy," where traditional investment rules did not apply.

Why is this time not different? The simple fact is that we are still faced with challenges and un-certainties, both in the outside world and here at home, that we still cannot see the future, and that many average, everyday people are still un-sure of how to invest their money. Many of these individuals need a steady hand to help guide their financial affairs, someone who can provide context and perspective to today's challenging questions.

We do not know what the stock market will do this year or next, or what decisions will be made at the next meeting of the Federal Reserve. We cannot anticipate when or if the United States will be attacked again by terrorists or when our involvement in Iraq will be brought to an end.

However, we do not need to know these things to invest money properly. Investment de-cisions should be based on investment princi-ples, not predictions. We continue to believe that staying focused on the key investment principles of diversification, buying quality investments, and maintaining a long-term perspective is the best way for investors to reach their long-term goals. Investors must understand the importance of being patient, and to be realistically optimistic regarding the long-term future of our country and the stock market. They should also know that the four most dangerous words in the world of investing are "This time is different."

Sy Sternberg

**Chairman and Chief Executive Officer,
New York Life Insurance Company**

Have the courage to be the first one in. Whether you are a buyer or seller, you don't want to be among the multitudes. It's those who come to market early, ahead of the crowd, who realize the greatest profit. Being the first in provides better returns. This is true in institutional investing, where being in the first tranche of an offering provides better returns. It's what drives the venture capital industry, where the risks assumed in investing in new enterprises are offset by the rewards of getting in on the ground floor with a winner.

I've found that the "first in" rule applies to personal financial decisions as well. When my family and I were looking for a new home, our real estate agent gave me a tip on a new development that had just come on the market: seven oversize lots, each with an equally oversize price. I said the cost was too high; she said, "Make an offer anyway." I later realized the seller needed a "bell cow"—a high-profile buyer to be the first in and entice his more cautious prospects. After he agreed to accept 35 percent less than what subsequent buyers would pay, I was convinced: It's good to be the bell cow!

Being first in requires the confidence to act quickly. My teenage son accompanied me on a car-shopping trip a few years ago. I'm a fan of two-door convertibles, but am not fond of soft tops. So, when I saw the new 2003 Mercedes SL500 roadster—with a retractable steel roof—my decision was simple. I asked the salesman how much. "We are asking $10,000 over sticker." "Fine," I said. "When can you have it ready?" My son's jaw dropped. (He knows I am not one to overpay.) Two weeks later, when we returned to pick up the car, he learned why I leaped so fast. The dealer had the only three SL500s in the state. All had sold. Following us, buyer #2 paid a $15,000 premium. Buyer #3 paid a $20,000 premium. And buyer #4 would have to wait at least eighteen months to take delivery!

If a deal doesn't meet your personal comfort threshold, don't even consider it. But if it does meet your requirements, don't hesitate. It's a good bet your decision will prove to be a better one now than later.

DAVID SWENSEN

**Chief Investment Officer,
Yale University Endowment Fund**

Charlie Ellis's book *Winning the Loser's Game* had a profound effect on me. The thrust of what he advises is that index funds ought to form the core of a portfolio. This is based on the notion that the market return is a very tough hurdle to beat—if you're going to attempt it, you are going to have to be partners with somebody who can reliably beat the market—that is a very difficult thing to do.

You need to be in the market day in and day out, and you need to be in a *variety* of markets day in and day out, not just the U.S. stock market—it is too volatile. Exposure to emerging markets is the spice that makes the stew interesting. Having a 5 or 10 percent allocation to emerging markets in Asia, perhaps Africa, the Middle East, Central Europe, and Latin America makes an enormous amount of difference—but don't get carried away. Put some in U.S. stock, put some in European stock, put some in Asian stock, put some in emerging markets stock, own some real estate, and pepper all of that with inflation index funds and traditional bonds. Spread it around and diversify. Get out there and be exposed.

Unfortunately, all the sources of help in navigating the investment world are conflicted. For example, you go to a broker to help you but the broker makes money if you turn your portfolio. A good source of low-cost, independent advice is very difficult to find, so people need to just roll up their sleeves and read the books that will give them a template to follow.

Chasing performance is the biggest mistake people make. Buying a hot fund, a fund that has already gone up, is a frequent mistake. Individuals do it overwhelmingly and consistently—it is very damaging to returns. Dollar-weighted returns, which take into account cash flows in and out of the fund, are invariably lower than the time-weighted returns because individuals buy high, after it has gone up, and then they sell low, after they have been disappointed by the performance. People should dollar-cost-average and should not pay attention to past performance numbers when making their allocations.

Unfortunately, people generally pick mutual

funds based on past performance—the adver-
tisements that the mutual fund industry puts in
the financial press reinforce that. The whole environment reinforces the idea that you should
buy something that has gone up, but from an investment perspective there is nothing that tells us
that things that have gone up are expected to
continue to go up. If anything, it is a perverse indicator. People should stop chasing performance
and just put together a sensible portfolio regardless of the ups and downs of the market.

JAMES TISCH

**President and Chief Executive Officer,
Loews Corporation**

"When there's nothing to do, do nothing."

That advice seems simple enough, but very few people seem to follow it. Investors generally feel the need to constantly make buy and sell decisions, as if they were investment action-junkies. For many investors, securities trading is a form of amusement, a way to pass the time, almost like a real-life video game or the blackjack table. Securities brokers feed into this urge for action for a very simple reason: They are compensated according to the number of transactions that they execute on behalf of their clients. But the action-junkie investor usually does not have good results because there are few really good investment opportunities of which one can take advantage in any given year. The big trick is to sit back, avoid the urge for action and amusement, and invest only when all the pieces add up to a solid investment idea. At all other times, pretend that you have asbestos-lined pockets: Don't let your money burn a hole in them!

JASON R. TRENNERT

**Chief Investment Strategist and
Senior Managing Director, International
Strategy and Investment Group, Inc.**

At ISI, I've had the good fortune of working for
some of the smartest people in the investment
business, including Ed Hyman, ranked the
number one economist in the country by *Institutional Investor* for a remarkable twenty-six
years, and Jim Moltz, former chairman and chief
investment strategist of C. J. Lawrence and now
vice chairman of ISI. When I first became the
firm's investment strategist, I asked Jim what
had allowed him to remain such a good market
forecaster for so many years. Jim was too
modest to even accept the premise of the question, but he said, "I think it's important to remain as intellectually flexible as possible. *And
remember, when the crowd gets strident about
their view, go the other way.*"

Jim's advice came in handy in the early days of March 2003, with the market about to retest the October 2002 lows and market bulls on the run. At the time, I gave a presentation to a large and storied investment management company that had just started a group of hedge funds. Despite the market's weakness at the time, I was bullish, believing that earnings would surprise people on the upside and, perhaps more important, that the underlying sentiment on stocks was discounting the worst-case scenario for the economy and America's involvement in Iraq. I pointed out the extreme levels of bearishness in our survey of hedge funds, twenty rather stern-looking men and women, sitting around a large oak conference table. I said, "Our survey shows there are a lot of people on the short side already. We think that if you're short, you may want to be careful. And if you're long—"

A young man, probably in his thirties, cut me off. He'd come to the meeting late and wanted to assert some control over its content. He was one of the new hedge fund managers and was obviously short. "Let me ask you a question," he said. "Where are all the smart people in this business?"

I was dumbfounded. At my company we have an unwritten rule that describing yourself as "smart" or substituting your own judgment for the market's was the next best thing to a necktie party. Before I could construct some meager response, he answered for me. "They're at hedge funds, my friend. So I think your firm's little index is going to be a good *leading* indicator rather than a good *contrarian* one. Stocks are going down."

The response around the table was a stunned silence punctuated only by furtive glances at me to see if I had already started to gather my things. I limped home to finish my prepared remarks and left. With the market making new lows, I wasn't quite sure my new friend wasn't entirely correct in his own assessment of his own intelligence and my own stupidity. I then remembered Jim's advice to go opposite to stridently held views. The sentiment and valuation disciplines we had established were telling us that the market was poised for a rally, and thanks to Jim's advice, I stuck with that view. Although I endured another week of pain, the S&P bottomed on March 11th, and went on to post a 28 percent total return in 2003. Going against the crowd is never easy, but perhaps Mark Twain put it best when he said, "It ain't what you know that gets you in trouble. It's what you know for sure that just ain't so." There is no better advice I know for success in the markets.

DONALD J. TRUMP

**Real Estate Entrepreneur,
Best-selling Author, and Television Producer**

My father told me that anything that seems too good to be true most likely is. That was sage advice, an old saying that has been around for a while because it deserves to be around for a while. It has been good advice when it comes to business, investment, everything in fact. My father was cautious and thorough, and when it came to investment and how much risk to assume, he would ask, "How much money can you stand to lose?" which is a commonsense way to approach investment of any sort. These two bits of advice work well together and can create a safety check when it comes to investment.

DON WASHKEWICZ

Chairman and Chief Executive Officer,
Parker Hannifin Corporation

The U.S. stock market has averaged over 10 percent annual growth since its inception. If you are an individual investing without professional help, it's important to diversify. My advice is put your money in an S&P 500 index fund and you should minimize your risk and realize acceptable returns. Over the long term, the S&P 500 has outperformed most funds. I've always been cautious about investing in individual foreign stocks or international funds holding foreign companies you know nothing about. Many of these funds have not perfomed well over the long term. My advice on "international" investing is that you will get plenty of exposure to international markets by investing in the S&P 500 index funds or broad-based equity funds, since many of these companies do

business globally. This approach should minimize your risk.

Note: You don't need to invest in foreign
stocks to get foreign exposure.

Lastly, we are very proud that Parker Hannifin Corporation has historically outperformed
the S&P 500 in total return.

ROBERT WEISSENSTEIN

**Chief Investment Officer,
Credit Suisse Private Banking USA**

When I first got into this business, my father, who is a photographer, thought I was going into the gambling industry. When I heard his reaction, I was determined to bring some discipline into the process. I viewed it as the most straightforward business. My job was to find great opportunities and make some money off of them.

Investing is not an academic exercise. You can learn whatever you want from books, but there is no replacement for spending time in the markets over a period of years to really learn how to handle yourself. Figuring out how to manage your money is an expertise that takes a great deal of focus and a lot of time. Investing has become an increasingly complex area in terms of understanding what is going on, not just in the markets but also in understanding how to gain exposure to different markets and investments. By hiring an advisor or financial planner, you aren't giving up your responsibility to understand what they are telling you and what they are advising you to do. You should never completely disconnect and you should not take advice at face value from a single person.

Over the years, I have frequently heard the statement, *This time it's different.* However, the reality is that it is rarely ever *that* different. People usually say this to justify extremes in the market. During the tech bubble, the only way you could make money was by investing in technology and everyone thought the whole world was going in a new direction. It was bothering me that the markets were continuing in such an extreme measure. No matter how much you spoke to investors about maintaining their discipline and remembering to stay diversified, they were getting more and more concentrated in tech investments.

The reality was that even though we were making great strides from a tech standpoint, it didn't mean that everything from the past was suddenly thrown out the window. This concept was made very clear to me the day the Nasdaq hit 5,000. Television reporters were apoplectically predicting when it was going to reach 6,000. I was in Hong Kong at the time and someone said to me, "Of course it's great that the world is changing and the technological advances are enormous right now, but what about companies like Colgate? What are we going to do, start using virtual toothpaste?" Some things are actually going to still be around. When you hear, *This time it's different*, you need to be very careful. This doesn't mean you shouldn't force yourself to think about things differently. Things do evolve. The ways that you can invest in the market evolve so you have to stay fresh. You can't say everything that worked before is going to be exactly what you do going forward.

U.S. investors tend to be fairly focused on U.S. markets because they are large and well capitalized with a lot of liquidity, but the reality is if you look at equity market capitalization globally the U.S. constitutes only half of what is going on. If you don't look outside your domestic market you are basically saying, *I'm not interested in half the opportunities out there*. You can't exclude an entire opportunity set like that. It doesn't always mean it is going to be great, but you have to at least look at it.

Diversification, a term often used in describing a successful investment strategy, means a portfolio that is not concentrated in one particular security. People are tempted to try to hit a home run because they hear stories about great investment success. But the more people try to hit a home run, the less likely they are to get on base. First, start with the concept that you need to be globally diversified. The barriers have come down, the opportunities are out there, and the markets are better capitalized. Second, there are a number of different asset classes out there and a portfolio should typically include equities and fixed income. There are a number of new instruments that allow you to get different types of exposure. Look into them. Hedge funds, foreign currency exposure, and structured notes, which give you a level of built-in downside protection with different levels of upside potential, are all worth considering for a well-diversified portfolio.

The classic question that people ask investors is *What is your risk tolerance?* This question is really asking *How much money are you willing to lose?* Nobody wants to lose, so the right question is *What is your acceptable level of volatility?* What kind of swings in your portfolio can you handle? The key is making sure you can withstand the volatility in order to let your portfolio do what it is supposed to do. If you don't figure out your volatility budget, you will not have a successful investing experience. You will get scared out of what you were supposed to do in the first place. Take tomorrow's market out of it, step back, understand your volatility level, let your portfolio do its job, and you will be better able to navigate through the more difficult environments and situations.

MILES WHITE

Chairman and Chief Executive Officer, Abbott Laboratories

Sports columnist Blackie Sherrod once wrote: "If you bet on a horse, that's gambling. If you bet you can make three spades, that's entertainment. If you bet cotton will go up three points, that's business. See the difference?"

Too many people forget that picking stocks is a lot like gambling. It's important to recognize that and understand that your strategy has to be about improving your odds—by informing your decisions with the right kind of information. There are three things I always look at to improve my odds as an investor: business model, earnings potential, and management.

First, a company needs a logical business model. I should be able to understand the basic premise of the company relatively quickly: what is the product, how is it made, who are the customers, and what are all the pieces in between?

Second, there needs to be a coherent path to generating not just revenue—but also earnings. A company can have a great-sounding concept—even one that will generate revenue—but if it isn't going to produce earnings, it's probably not going to be a good investment. That should be obvious, but too many investors seem to ignore that aspect of business reality and dive in at the top line.

Third, and most important, the management team needs to have what it takes to win. That means they need to be willing to take risks, but not make them. It means they need to have a long-term view of their business. (I don't invest in any management team that appears more concerned about quarterly earnings than where their company will be in five years.) They also need to have a fundamental understanding that success in the marketplace is a form of winning. Business is competition and you need a game plan that aims for the win.

It should be fairly straightforward getting the information you need in order to make an informed investment decision—because companies are, in a sense, competing for our investment dollars. If I can't get enough information on these criteria, I move on to the next opportunity.

Maybe it's because I grew up in Las Vegas, but I never stop considering that picking a stock—or any investment vehicle—is like placing a bet. With the right information, however, and the homework to get it, you can make a better-informed gamble with improved odds of a positive payout.

C. JOHN WILDER

Chairman and Chief Executive Officer, TXU Corporation

"Buy low; sell high."
—UNKNOWN

TIM WOLF

**Global Chief Financial Officer,
Molson Coors Brewing Company**

Point 1: Focus on this stuff at least once a quarter. Very frequently I see people with a lot of money who are just too busy—too busy making money and they spend very little time preserving or protecting or building what they've got. Most people don't really understand what their risk profile is. Most people don't ask themselves with enough fastidiousness, *Am I the sort of investor who really, really loves to be uncomfortable, or do I really want to sleep at night?*

I think that many investors talk as though they are more than willing to take on risk, but when they're talking about it they are not internalizing the fact they are just looking for the reward from that risk, not the risk itself. This is hard for people to understand unless they've been burned pretty badly. Constantly test your

own, and your family's, perception of what sort
of risk-reward relationship makes sense. It's a really hard thing to do on your own. Use your
spouse, friend, or investment advisor. You need
to test it a lot, especially if you've got a new job,
or a windfall, or you are thinking of retiring.
You sometimes see very smart people with good
educations making a lot of money and they go
bust. How does this happen? They put all their
money on red 21 or XYZ stock.

Point 2: At any age, whether twenty or fifty,
be mindful of how you allocate assets. Always
have a portfolio of your investments that are
risk-free, and as you get older reassess that percentage of risk-free investment.

Point 3: Diversify. Never get greedy. Most
people say it but few practice it. The notion of
buying an equity and having a target price and
holding to your target price is really a silly notion because you are presuming a lot of knowledge and a lot of insight that you need to
develop a target price. Instead, think about a return in the period of time you're looking at. If
you get a 3 percent return in one quarter, and it
continues at that rate, that's more than 12 percent for the year. Most people would take that
and run.

Think about the riskiness, especially of the equity investments you make. Save something. The
definition of save to me is an investment with a

low risk profile. Save something every quarter. Don't wait to do this when you're forty, fifty, or sixty or when you get a raise. To me this is something like basic hygiene, like brushing your teeth and working out—there's a consistency of applying an investment discipline that I think most people forget.

What you preach to your kids is good advice for investors at any age. In our house, our formula with our kids is ⅓, ⅓, ⅓: ⅓ you can spend, ⅓ you should save, and ⅓ you should give away. Those percentages don't always work out but they are a good basis to follow.

STEPHEN P. ZELDES

**Benjamin Rosen Professor of Economics
and Finance, Columbia Business School**

My grandfather Nathaniel E. Stein was a stockbroker in New York City. In 1966, when I was nine years old, he consulted carefully with me and then bought me my first shares of stock. We purchased a few shares of IBM, Xerox, and Tootsie Roll. I followed the stock prices carefully. Within a few weeks of our purchase, one of the stocks had fallen in value, and I dashed him off a postcard from a lakeside vacation spot in New Hampshire. "Dear Mr. Stein," the postcard read. "Deeply disturbed about Xerox. Please advise. I've lost $15.00 already. Your customer, Stephen Paul Zeldes."

When I returned from vacation, I was surprised and pleased to receive in the mail a five-paragraph handwritten letter from my grandfather. (His response, together with my original postcard, were found many years later and are now framed and hanging on my wall. What follows is an excerpt of his letter.) "Dear Mr. Zeldes," he began. "Referring to your succinct and terse postcard, I regret to learn that you are 'disturbed' about the loss in your holding of Xerox. However, since this is your first venture into the intricacies of finance, you should be aware that stocks do not go up all the time. The purchase of your Xerox was made because you wanted to have an investment that would 'grow.' The word grow means that each successive three months your company would sell more products, and make higher profits, than the preceding three months. You will note that I bought for you 25 shares of Tootsie Roll at 13⅝. This is down from 22 and I believe that the product will be in ever growing demand as time goes on. As to Xerox, while the stock is down you should not be disturbed, but be audacious— and buy more. The reason for holding a stock is that you believe in the future of the company. If you don't believe this, then you should sell.

"With kindest personal regards—and a hope that I might merit your future confidence and business—I remain, Sincerely, Nathaniel E. Stein."

While Xerox did not turn out to have particularly good long-term payoffs (I should have sold it when I wrote the postcard), the wisdom and advice from my grandfather did. What I gleaned most from my grandfather in this realm was a trust in the workings of and the importance of investing in the stock market. Back in the 1960s, when I took my first tentative steps into the world of investing, only a quarter of U.S. households held stocks of any kind, either directly or indirectly through mutual funds. I was fortunate to learn early about the merits of stockownership and to be a part of that 25 percent. I learned from my grandfather that investing in the stock market was risky ("stocks do not go up all the time"), but that over the long haul, investing in a well-diversified portfolio of stocks was likely to pay off. I also certainly owe part of my subsequent interest in and curiosity about financial markets and economics to the time I spent talking with my grandfather.

The fraction of households involved in some way in the stock market rose substantially in the 1980s and 1990s to a level just over 50 percent today. Much of this was due to the dramatic change in the pension landscape over the last twenty-five years: We have seen a marked decline in the prevalence of defined benefit pension plans and a huge rise in the prevalence of defined contribution plans. As a result of this change, the financial responsibility people have to take for their own retirement has greatly increased. It is more important than ever for individuals to have a strong grasp of financial fundamentals.

The following are some basic steps that I think people should take in order to increase their chances of investment success:

1. Start saving and investing when you are young. A surprising number of people do not participate in their 401(k) plans. Don't make that mistake.

2. Invest a significant amount of your overall wealth in the stock market. Understand that the stock market is risky, but that for most people the added expected return should make it a good bet.

3. Diversification is crucial. A well-diversified portfolio is integral to long-term investing success. This is best achieved by holding stocks in a large number of companies in diverse sectors or by holding mutual funds that track broad indices. Also, a common mistake that people make is to hold large amounts of their own company's stock. By doing this, your overall portfolio is less diversified, and since you already have a stake by working in the company, you are vulnerable on many fronts if the company performs poorly. Your salary may decrease or your job may disappear at

the same time that your financial position in the company's stock is diminished—and this is financially dangerous. Enron drove home this point to an extreme degree and it is worth remembering. If you aren't a high-level executive who is forced to hold company stock, it is generally better to avoid doing so.

4. Do not be afraid of foreign markets. Investing in them will enhance a well-diversified portfolio. Because they are not perfectly correlated with U.S. markets, holding a broad basket of stocks from other countries will, over the long run, enable you to get higher average returns with lower risk.

5. Timing the market and picking individual stocks is extremely difficult. There are some people who have done very well at this, but there are far more who have done poorly, especially after factoring in commissions and other trading costs. The casual investor is better off not doing it, but instead buying equity index funds with low expenses and fees.

6. Finally, boost your financial literacy as much as possible. Read the articles on personal finance and basic macroeconomics that appear in *The Wall Street Journal* and *The New York Times*. When MBA students finish my macroeconomics class at Columbia Business School,

one of the things that I hope they are walking away with is the ability to read and understand those articles. Never underestimate the importance of financial literacy.

ABOUT THE AUTHOR

LIZ CLAMAN is an Emmy Award–winning, internationally recognized television news anchor and journalist. Throughout her career, she has covered local, national, and world events for CBS, ABC, and NBC affiliates in Los Angeles; Columbus and Cleveland, Ohio; and Boston. For the past eight years, she has anchored at CNBC, hosting the cable business network's shows *Wake Up Call*, *Morning Call*, *Market Wrap*, and *Cover to Cover*. A graduate of UC Berkeley and Université Paris–Sorbonne, Claman, an avid runner, ran the New York City marathon in November 2005. She resides in Edgewater, New Jersey, with her husband and two children.

215